i

Thus Saith God's Word; Scripture Aids for Counseling

Dorothy Mason Weymann

KINGDOM CREATION PUBLISHERS©
Spartanburg, SC

Printed in Charleston, SC by CreateSpace; On-
Demand Publishing LLC.
CreateSpace
4900 LaCross Road
North Charleston, SC 29406

Published in the United States of America

Thus Saith God's Word

<u>**DEDICATION**</u>

This book is also written in memory of my father, JAMES WESLEY MASON, who was dedicated to God's service before he was born. In his 90 years, he never once used liquor, tobacco, vice of any form, nor evil communications.

"I have chosen you and ordained you that you should go and bring forth fruit." (John 15:16).

After Jesus baptized him with His Holy Spirit in 1932, he both "went" and "brought forth fruit." All the gifts of the Spirit were manifested through him as he proclaimed the "good news" of the "full gospel" of Jesus Christ in the pulpit, in prisons and to needy individuals wherever he found them, in America and also in Mexico, where the Lord called him to labor for Him.

Together we founded the Good News Recording Company that carried the word in Spanish and English throughout the world by means of radio and the written page.

In his later years he became a legend: people of all races and from every walk of life came to him day and night and were saved, baptized in the Spirit, healed, delivered from bondage and reconciled one to another. Jesus said: "Follow me and I will make you fishers of men." My father was one of God's great fishermen, and I loved him.

~Dorothy Mason Weymann

<u>NOTE CONCERNING COVER PICTURE:</u>

The blue glass pitcher, a wedding gift from the owner of a Mexican glass factory, had always been admired for its shape and color. Years later, it was with great consternation that I saw it knocked from a shelf and fall to the floor. On bended knee and with tears flowing, I searched for the many scattered pieces, then painstakingly glued them together - all but one lost piece. It was after this that I made the painting. Because of my determination, its beauty has not been lost and is now giving a testimony for the Water of Life as this book goes around the world.

No one should consider his or her life as being beyond help, no matter how broken or seemingly useless, but instead let Jesus put it together again. Given the ingredients of determination, true repentance and complete surrender, God will make something beautiful out of any life - a vessel from which He can pour out His "Living Water" to others. Jesus knows where even the one lost piece is. He is the "Good Shepherd" who goes in search of the "one lost sheep."

May God richly bless you as you utilize this tool in your efforts to proclaim His Salvation.

THE PURPOSE OF THIS BOOK

THE PURPOSE OF THIS BOOK is to tell ALL people EVERYWHERE that the God of all creation is a GOD of LOVE and that everything He designed and made was for the good and happiness of the people He created in His own image and likeness. The SPECIAL BEAUTY of our PLANET EARTH was not by chance but was planned by an Intelligence far beyond human intellect and whose laws of nature, physics, gravity, electricity, etc. are ageless and changeless.

GOD, Who is invisible to human eye, has not tried to hide from mankind - instead, has revealed Himself everywhere, from the splendors of the heavens to the uniqueness and magnificence of the earth and from the marvels of the human body and mind to the mysteries of the atom. He is not a God made from wood, stone, clay or metal by the hands of man but a GOD who HEARS, SEES and KNOWS all things and is all powerful, yet desires to have personal fellowship with every man, woman and child in the world. He loves each one individually. You, DEAR READER, are important to God for He loves you. YOU ARE SPECIAL!

It is man, through disobedience, who has separated himself from this Holy God and has worshipped the created objects instead of the Creator. God, however, has given us His Book of Instructions, the Bible, that we might know His requirements for finding our way back to Him and to have on oeeeptable, happy life on this earth and acceptance into His Eternal Kingdom after this earthly sojourn.

His Word was given "that we may know we have eternal life," and that upon leaving this world, we will be welcomed by Jesus Himself saying: "Come, ye blessed of my Father, inherit the kingdom prepared for you from the foundation of the world."

"Eye has not seen, nor ear heard, neither has entered into the heart of man, the things which God has prepared for them that love him." There will be indescribable flowers and wondrous trees growing beside a sparkling, pure river of the water of life, clear as crystal. Every moment will bring new wonders and nothing will ever become monotonous. There will be no sin, no sickness, no doctors, no dentists, no ambulances, hospitals or asylums and no funerals. No liars or thieves or drunkards will be there; no jealousy, gossip or hatred; and wars shall be no more. Nobody will ever grow old and nothing will decay. After a thousand centuries all will be as young and as fresh as at the beginning.

"The Lord is not willing that any should perish" for He has prepared a place where eternal peace and joy will flow like a river forever, and FOREVER is a long, L-O-N-G time! Multiply all the grains of sand in all the seas by all the leaves on all the trees then by all the stars in all the galaxies. Count this number in years and ETERNITY WILL JUST HAVE BEGUN!

Dorothy Mason Weymann

Thus Saith God's Word

Thus Saith God's Word

Dorothy Mason Weymann

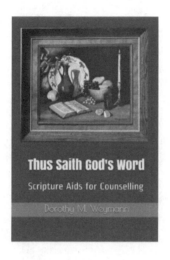

KINGDOM CREATION PUBLISHERS©
Spartanburg, SC

Thus Saith God's Word

TABLE OF CONTENTS

Dedication...vi

Note Concerning Cover picture:...........................viii

The Purpose of This Book ix

You Shall Know the Truth and the Truth Shall Set
You Free 6

Abortion..12

Alcohol 15

Answers to Critics...10

Backsliding 18

Comfort..22

Covenants 24

Cults/ Occult 27

Death- Life After Death......................................33

Discouragement 42

Drugs..45

Eternal Safety...49

Evolution..56

Faith 59

False Religions..64

Family 13

Fear 72

Finances 76

Forgiveness- Guilt 81

Guidance 85

Healing..89

Holiness 100

Holy Spirit 103

    Who is the Holy Spirit?................................103
    The Holy Spirit Through the Bible 105
    Baptism (Gifts)..120
    Results of the Baptism...............................123

Jews...128

    God's Redemptive Plan for the World.........128

Loneliness 150

Marriage...155

Obedience 168

Peace 170

Prayer...173

Protection...176

Sacraments 180

Salvation 183

    Jesus- Our High Priest.................................191
    The Christian's Declaration Of Independence 195
    Test of a True Believer...............................197

Sleep 199

Second Coming...203

Sexual Sins...219

    Adultery...220
    Fornication 221
    Perversion..221
    Pornography 223
Smoking..226

Suicide 230

Thoughts 235

Word of God...240

What is the True Purpose for Life?......................248

<u>YOU SHALL KNOW THE TRUTH AND THE TRUTH SHALL SET YOU FREE</u>

Where can we find the basic point from which we can establish truth? It must come from the beginning of all things. No place can we find definite statements of the beginning except in the divine, indestructible, inerrant Word of God - The Bible. (See "<u>Word of God</u>") It is the Official Rule Book. Thus, everything must be judged "true" or "false" according to its tenets.

The prime test of conformity to the "Rule Book" is: "What think you of Jesus?" as He is the central theme of every book in the Bible. Isaiah prophesied, *"For unto us a child is born, unto us a son is given... and His name shall be called Wonderful, Counsellor, The Mighty God."* John declared Him to be the "Word" and *"the Word was God... and the Word was made flesh." "By Him were all things created that are in heaven, and that are in earth, visible and invisible and by Him all things consist."*

Isaiah 43:11 says: *"I, even I AM THE LORD and beside me THERE IS NO SAVIOUR."* The annunciation of the angel of the Lord to the shepherds was "For unto you is born this day in the city of David, a Savior which is Christ the Lord."

Therefore, it is clearly and definitely established that Jesus was God in the flesh - the second person of the Triune Godhead - God the Father, God the Son, and God the Holy Spirit. Jesus declared it Himself: *"I and my Father are one... <u>The Lord possessed me in the beginning</u> of His way, before His works of old. I was set*

6

up from everlaster. When He prepared the heavens, I WAS THERE... I was daily His delight, rejoicing always before him. (**Prov. 8:22-30**).

Jesus spoke of the Third person of the Trinity as "the Spirit of Truth," "the Comforter" and "when He is come He will reprove the world of sin, righteousness and judgment." "He will guide you into all truth."

The word for God in Hebrew is"*Elohim*" which is PLURAL but is always used with a SINGULAR VERB and occurs 2,310 times in the Bible. "*Hear, O Israel, the Lord our God is one (echod) God.*" (Deut.6:4) Why mention the name of God 3 times --for each one of the Trinity. There are two words for one, "*yachid*" a solitary one and "echod" a united one. The spies brought back one (echod) cluster of grapes from Canaan- many grapes but one cluster. (Each grape has 3 parts -the skin, flesh, seed.) "All the people.(400,000 men) arose as one (ECHOD) man."

Examples of the Trinity are on all sides.All colors are made from the 3 primary colors; no musical key can be established without 3 tones; all time is divided into 3 parts-past, present and future; all life exists in either the air, the land, or the water. Water, the sustainier of life itself made up of 3 parts: 2 parts hydrogen and 1 part oxygen - and can be in 3 forms - solid, liquid and vapor; yet it is all water - a perfect example of the Trinity. Each has His own form and office but are ONE GOD.

(1x1x1=1)

7

It being clearly established that Jesus is God and He called Himself "the Truth," HE CANNOT LIE. His words are indisputable and He said: "No man comes to the Father BUT BY ME. He that hears my word and believes on Him that sent me has everlasting life and shall not come into condemnation but is passed from death unto life." (John 5 : 2 4) "He that believeth not the Son shall not see life; but the wrath of God abideth on him… These shall go away into everlasting punishment." (John 3:36; Matt. 25:46).

THERE IS A HELL – God Himself said so and it has flames. It is a place of everlasting punishment and of weeping and gnashing of teeth and torment.

Jesus also said **THERE IS A DEVIL**: "I behld Satan as lighting fall from heaven.: (Luke 10:18). As "the Prince of this world," – "Prince of the power of the air," he has assumed the position of god- substitute for this world. People are not consciously aware of Satan as their god. What he is concerned about is that they should not turn to the only God by the way of the cross of Jesus, so he throws a veil of darkness over men's minds and often makes the evil course appear good. He and his ministers often pose as being on the side of righteousness, or appearing as inspired prophets.

He lays traps and the property of a trap is that it appears to be normal and good until it is sprung. He is a foe to be reckoned with! His main concern is to divert us into alterna-tives to the gospel of Jesus in the form of plausible psychic and spiritual experiences. These are the check points so you can recognize his traps:

8

FIRST, that the Bible in its entirety is the word of God and the only true and necessary authority on His will. "Know this first, that no prophecy of the scripture is of any private interpretation." (2 Pet. 1:20). Stay as close as possible to the original, not private trans-lations, man's interpretations or paraphrases.

SECOND, check as to whether or not Jesus was God in the flesh, the only begotten Son of God the Father;. not a Son of God, or even the Son but not actually God; and with the father from the beginning-not just a "thought!'

THIRD,anyone,or anything that denies a literal hell where those who have not accepted Jesus as Savior are punished forever, is of Satan. If there is no eternal hell, Jesus is a liar and every birth certificate, every legal document, every business transaction, every postmark on every letter, every license plate, every news-paper and every magazine around the world is dated from the birth of the biggest liar who ever lived. THIS CANNOT POSSIBLY BE SO!

During the centuries, a deceiver could not have been the INSPIRATION for masterpieces of art , beautiful music, hospitals, schools and orphanages as well as the theme for millions of literary works! He could not have been revered for two thousand years by millions of people as the Bread of Life; the Bright and Morning Star;the Chief Shepherd;the Everlasting Father;the Holy One of God; King of Glory; Lamb of God;Light of the World; Lily of the Valley; the Great Physi-cian; the Prince of Peace; Redeemer; the Word of

Life and the Saviour of the World.

"THE FOOL HATH SAID IN HIS HEART, THERE IS NO GOD." (**Psa. 14:1**)

Who but a FOOL can put clothes on his back, shoes on his feet,awatch on his wrist, a ring on his finger; live in a house, ride in a car and fly in an airplane--none of which came in-to existance without a designer and maker--and yet say that his body -- with its billions of cells, organs, tissues, elevators, conveyors, cooling systems, refineries, communication and filing systems, etc. - came into being by chance without a Designer and Creator?

Who gave the human tongue flexibility to form words, and a brain to understand them, but denied it to all the animals? Who taught the kidneys how to filter poison from the blood and leave good things alone? How does it know one from the other?

Who put the sun and the moon in the sky? Who started the earth to spin at a given speed with-out ever slowing up - giving day and night-and tilting it to give seasons; and who put the magnetic poles into place?

Who declared that water should expand when it freezes, while other substances contract, thus making ice lighter than water, floating on the surface so that lakes wouldn't freeze solid and all the fish die?

Who devised fire and who made electricity? Who invented wave lengths for sound to travel on?

Where did the seeds come from for the first tree, the first flower, the first vegetable? Who designed the lily; who chose the perfume of the rose; the flavor of the grape, and the color of the beet? How have the shapes, perfumes, colors and flavors stayed constant for thousands of years? Who made pole-climbing beans north of the equator righthanded while those south of the e-quator lefthanded?

Who but an all-knowing God could cause a man to write down exactly what would happen over 2,500 years later to a nation that had ceased to officially exist? (Eze,36:24, 34-36; 37:21,11) and to foretell the present-day lineup of countries; what their plans would be as well as the outcome. The WISE man says:"Great is the Lord... My God!"

ABORTION

The male egg moment cell, one the male command sperm cell is given fertilizes to begin the unbelievable construction of a human life. It is as if an army of skilled engineers, chemists, computer experts, etc. immediately start to work without a supervisor et each knowing exactly when to come "on the job" and when to stop; working silently and in the dark; drawing from physical and character traits from a long line of ancestors.
God is not preparing a "tumor" (fetus) that WILL BECOME a HUMAN BEING upon CONTACT with fresh air and light, but IS CREATING a DESIGNED INDIVIDUAL, different from anyone who has ever lived or will live. Few realize that a heart beat is detectable at 18 DAYS; brain waves measurable at 43 DAYS; all systems are formed by 8 WEEKS; all functioning at 11 WEEKS and except for size, by 20 WEEKS the child is virtually developed.

- **Psa, 139; 13-16**- "You have covered me in my mother's womb. I will praise You, for I am fearfully and wonderfully made; My substance was not hid from You, when I was made in secret .. Your eyes saw my unformed bones and in Your book all my members were written…when as yet there was none of them."

The Lord said of Jeremiah: "Before I formed thee I knew thee; and before thou earnest out of the womb, I sanctified thee, and I ordained thee a prophet unto the nations." (Jer.1:5)

- **Ex. 20:13**- *Thou shalt not kill. (*murder) **Rev.21:8**. *murderers… shall have their part in the lake which burneth with fire and brimstone.*
- **Ex. 23:7**- *Never have any part in putting an innocent person to death. I will not justify anyone taking part in such wickedness.*

Many over ask: (1) "Doesn't a woman over have the right over her own body?" Yes, over her body: but the child is a completely separate human being with a genetic code that is entirely different from the mother's body cells. (2) With the overpopulation why bring another unwanted person into the world?" Many, many unwanted babes have become the object of great love and brought great blessing to the home. If a mother has the legal right to kill her unborn child, who is the social burden to her, could it not be just as logical for a child to kill his or her mother when later she becomes old and a social burden?

Present day society CONDONES SEXUAL PERMISSIVENESS which often leads to abortions but GOD JUDGES PERMISSIVENESS as SIN and ABORTION as MURDER. He commands to FLEE TEMPTATION. Don't get into situations that lead to promiscuous sex such as sex- oriented movies, reading sex books, dressing o entice, etc. Believe it or not, YOU will have to GIVE AN ACCOUNT of yourself BEFORE GOD. It takes TWO to make a baby and GOD holds BOTH ACCOUNTABLE for the child is being created in HIS IMAGE and BY HIS POWER.

No one gets away with sin. *"Whatsoever a man soweth, that shall he also reap."* (**Gal. 6:7**). *"Be sure your sin will find you out."* (**Num.32:23**).

If you have already done that which is wrong in God's sight but are truly repentant, sincerely desiring His forgiveness and cleansing and are willing to turn from your sins, go to Him., making complete confession and ask His forgiveness. He is waiting for you to come. He longs to hear you say you are truly sorry and He will gladly pardon you, free you from guilt, erase memories and give you a new start. (See "Salvation")

ALCOHOL

Alcohol destroys homes; turns ambitious youths into hopeless parasites; men into brutes; women into derelicts; destroys the weak and weakens the strong; and has killed more people than have fallen in all the wars of the world.

It is said alcoholism is a disease but the Bible says it 1s the result of SIN. One does not buy a disease by the bottle nor serve it for parties. Sickness will not keep a person out of heaven but alcohol will.

- **1 Cor. 6:10**- *No drunkard shall inherit the kingdom of God.*

Alcohol is by far the worst drug in the world as far as number of injured and killed is con-cerned. In this country it is fast becoming the No. #1 killer. It destroys brain cells that will never be replaced and seriously effects the heart and liver.

It temporarily impairs vision, speech and coordination as well as numbs inhibitions and guilt. People spend years and vast sums of money to obtain an education, gain social status, success in profession or business, ranks in the military, etc. and yet after a few drinks, are reduced to fools with less control over their mind and body than a kindergarten child.

In spite of all this, Americans spend 30 billion dollars a year on liquor as there are 100 million users; 28% of the children in grades 7 to 12 are "problem drinkers."

- **Ecc. 11:9**- *"Rejoice, O young man, in thy youth; and let thy heart cheer thee in the days of thy youth, and walk in the ways of thine heart, and in the sight of thine eyes: but know thou, that FOR ALL THESE THINGS GOD WILL BRING THEE INTO JUDGMENT.*

A person drinks NOT from THIRST but from EMPTINESS; but God's child has His promise: "My people shall be satisfied with my goodness. (Jer. 31:14).

There are many excuses for drinking:

worry-depression	relaxation
insecurity	escape from reality
inferiority	stimulant

Some drink due to loneliness, not knowing that Jesus is *"a Friend that sticketh closer than a brother."* (**Prov. 18:24**).

Many drink to cover guilt. God says, *"He that covereth his sin shall not prosper."* (**Prov. 28:13**).

Some serve alcoholic beverages because it is the 'gracious way to entertain,' but God says:

- **Hab. 2:15**- "*WOE unto him that giveth his neighbour drink, that puttest thy bottle to him, and makest him drunken also…*"

The vast majority drink because "everybody is doing it," and they fear being "different," Any inanimate object floats downstream; it takes life to go against the current.

- **1 John 5:12**- *"He that hath the Son hath Life."*

Daniel was a young captive in a foreign coun-try but he purposed in his heart not to DEFILE himself with the portion of the king's meat nor with the WINE.

- **Prov. 20:1**- *"Wine is a mocker, strong drink is raging: and whosoever is deceived thereby is not wise."*

- **Hos. 4:11**- *"Wine take away the heart."*

- **Prov. 23:29-32**- *"Who hath woe? who hath sorrow? who hath contentions? who hath babbling? who hath wounds without cause? who hath redness of eyes?They that tarry long at the wine; they that go to seek mixed wine. Look not thou upon the wine when it is red, when it giveth his colour in the cup, when it moveth itself aright. At the last it biteth like a serpent, and stingeth like an adder."*

- **Isa. 5:22**- *"Woe unto them that are mighty to drink wine, and men of strength to mingle strong drink:"*

The devil always corrupts that which is good. Grains that should be used to feed the starving of the world are being turned into liquor to enslave those who drink it.

The same is true of grapes that have a "blessing" in them (lsa.65:8) for they contain pure glucose which passes directly into the blood and goes to every cell in the body for its growth, development, division, and maintenance. Is it any wonder Jesus likened the "fruit of the vine" to His pure blood that He left heaven to give as a ransom for all mankind?

The Bible continually equates WINE with STRONG DRINK (Leviticus, Numbers, Judges, Proverbs, Isaiah, Micah and Luke) (10 oz. of beer=6 oz. of wine= ½ oz. of hard liquor) end pronounces a "WOE" (def. a heavy CALAMITY. a CURSE) on those who partake of them.

God is no respecter of persons. For His children He has but ONE STANDARD regardless of country, culture, and customs. He commands to: ABSTAIN from ALL APPEARANCE of EVIL." (1 Thess. 5:22).

- **2 Cor. 6: 17**- *"Wherefore come out from among them and be ye separate, saith the Lord, and TOUCH NOT the UNCLEAN THING; and I will receive you."*

Wine, beer and hard liquor come under both headings-- EVIL and UNCLEAN. God would not pro-nounce a WOE on the use of alcoholic beverages in the Old Testament and sanction it in the New. Any seeming contradiction is in the translation and/or interpretation. *"Let God be true, but every man a liar."* **(Rom,3:4)** *"The Lord is righteous in all His ways, and holy in all his works."* **(Psa. 145:17).**

Thus He would not approve of His children drinking anything that would rob them of clear thinking and slow down their reflexes even to the slightest degree and cause them to be a stumbling block to the "unsaved" who are being enslaved by it and are staggering their way to hell!

If you consider yourself in His family and have thought God would condemn the "unsaved" drinker and yet pass by you with approval, YOU HAVE BEEN MISGUIDED! You need to make confession and be forgiven and freed, that you "give no offence in any thing." (1 Cor.l0:3l-32; Mat. 18:6-9).

(Suggested Prayer)

DEAR GOD, I come to You for forgiveness and cleansing. I am sorry I did not realize I was being ensnared by the devil. Help me from this day on to recognize his traps. If I have caused any to go astray, give me the opportunity to redeem the false and give a true witness for You that You are my sufficiency in all things. I offer You my body as a living sacrifice. Help me to keep it holy and acceptable unto You and to the glory and honor of Jesus. Amen.

****

The alcoholic MUST ADMIT his or her need for help and that GOD, thru His Son JESUS, is the ONLY HELP. Admit that it is a SIN.

- **1 John 1:9-10**- *"If we confess out sins, He is faithful and just to forgive us our sins, and cleanse us from all unrighteousness."*

(Suggested Prayer)

DEAR LORD, I can't go on any longer; I tried my way - really the devil's way- and it has only brought me unhappiness and bondage. I NOW RENOUNCE all connection with him. Please break the chains that bind me and set me free from Satan's hold on my mind and my body- Take out all roots of desire for that which is contrary to Your will.

I acknowledge my sins and truly repent of them. Wash me clean with Your blood, Jesus, I accept You as my Savior. Walk with me; guide my steps into the paths of righteousness for Your name's sake. Put Your hand in mine, and may I never put anything else there that would bring You shame. Take my lips that nothing will pass them that would defile me or steal away my power of thinking. Restore my mind and may the words that proceed from my mouth be pleasing to You. I thank You for hearing this prayer and that You will change me from a loser to a winner. Help me to keep my eyes on You. Thank You for saving me. Amen.

After confessing your sins, accept the pardon and freedom He promises. "If the Son shall make you free, ye shall be free indeed." "Put ye on the Lord Jesus Christ, and make not provision for the flesh, to fulfill the lusts thereof."

DESTROY all liquor, drugs, tobacco, etc.; Buy no more, ACCEPT no more.

- **2 Cor. 5:17**- *Therefore, if any man be in Christ, he is a new creature; the old things are passed away; behold, all things are become new.*

No longer fellowship with sinful companions. Whosoever will be a friend of the world is an enemy of God.

- **Col. 3:10**- *If ye then be risen with Christ, seek those things which are above, where Christ sitteth on the right hand of God. ² Set your affection on things above, not on things on the*

5

earth. *³ For ye are dead, and your life is hid with Christ in God. ⁴ When Christ, who is our life, shall appear, then shall ye also appear with him in glory. ⁵ Mortify therefore your members which are upon the earth; fornication, uncleanness, inordinate affection, evil concupiscence, and covetousness, which is idolatry: ⁶ For which things' sake the wrath of God cometh on the children of disobedience: ⁷ In the which ye also walked some time, when ye lived in them. ⁸ But now ye also put off all these; anger, wrath, malice, blasphemy, filthy communication out of your mouth. ⁹ Lie not one to another, seeing that ye have put off the old man with his deeds; ¹⁰ And have put on the new man, which is renewed in knowledge after the image of him that created him.*

- **1 Cor. 6:20**- *For ye are bought with a price: therefore glorify God in your body and in your spirit, which are God's.*

- **Romans 12:1-2**- *I beseech you therefore, brethren, by the mercies of God that you present your bodies as a living sacrifice, acceptable unto God, which is your reasonable service. And be not conformed to this world...*

Stop all blaming of people or circumstances. Do not entertain self-pity. All things worked together to bring you to this moment of surrender. God has given you His best-His Son; now start giving Him your best! Praise Him constantly.

- **1 Pet. 5:8-9**- *Be sober, be vigilant; because your adversary the devil, as a roaring lion, walketh about, seeking whom he may devour: ⁹ Whom*

> *resist stedfast in the faith, knowing that the same afflictions are accomplished in your brethren that are in the world.*

Faith comes from the Word, study it daily and keep in constant contact with God by prayer. Jesus made provision that His followers have the same power He had as the Son of Man to overcome Satan. (See" Holy Spirit," also "Drugs" "Salvation" and "The Word of God.")

- **Col. 1:10**- *That ye might walk worthy of the Lord unto all pleasing... in every good work.*

Throughout the Bible TWO kinds of wine are spoken of: (]) bad wine that is poisonous and destructive -the cause of intoxication, of violence and woe; the use of which is punishable by eternal damnation; (2) good wine that was not intoxicating and was used as an offering to God; the emblem of spiritual blessings and of the blood of atonement.

Fermented wine is decayed juice. Jesus is the Author of LIFE, not corruption, and if He had changed water into fermented (decayed) wine at the wedding in Cana, then He would also have created moldy bread and rotten fish to feed the five thousand.

If the false accusation of His enemies that He was a "winebibber" is to be believed, (Mat. 1:1-19) then He was also "gluttonous" and "had a devil."(John 8: 48). These are NOT TRUE the "HOLY ONE of ISRAEL."

- **Eph. 5:18**- *Be not drunk with wine wherein is excess, but be filled with the Spirit.*

This is not a license to drink moderate amounts but a dire warning of its consequences. "Excess" means: "debauchery", R.S.V.; "incorrigibleness or riotous living", Thayer's Greek Lexicon. The same word is used in Luke 15: 13.

GAMES OF CHANCE

To play games is not bad in itself but to play games of chance to win money becomes a vice and people become "hooked" on them. The first hand of poker, the first racing bet, the first coin in a slot machine does not make a gambler but it is a seed planted that if cultivated, will grow out of control. Excuses are plentiful: "Just this time;" "Every body's doing it;" "All life is a gamble-everything depends on luck." NOT TRUE of a real Christian for: *"The steps of a righteous man are ordered of the Lord."* (**Psa. 37:23**).

Gambling and drinking go hand in hand. They are the devil's traps that cause the whole family to suffer; jobs to be lost, money used that should go to feed and clothe loved ones, and homes to break up.

- **1 Tim. 5:8**- *But if any provide not for his own, and specially for those of his own house, he hath denied the faith, and is worse than an infidel.*

- **Isa. 55:2-7**- *Wherefore do ye spend money for that which is not bread? and your labour for that which satisfieth not? hearken diligently unto me, and eat ye that which is good, and let your soul delight itself in fatness. ³ Incline your ear,*

*and come unto me: hear, and your soul shall
live; and I will make an everlasting covenant
with you, even the sure mercies of David.
[4] Behold, I have given him for a witness to the
people, a leader and commander to the people.
[5] Behold, thou shalt call a nation that thou
knowest not, and nations that knew not thee
shall run unto thee because of the LORD thy
God, and for the Holy One of Israel; for he hath
glorified thee. [6] Seek ye the LORD while he may
be found, call ye upon him while he is near: [7] Let
the wicked forsake his way, and the unrighteous
man his thoughts: and let him return unto
the LORD, and he will have mercy upon him; and
to our God, for he will abundantly pardon.*

ANSWERS TO CRITICS

1.   The experience on Pentecost was only for that
     day to show that the Holy Spirit was given to the
     Jews and at Cornelius' house He was given to
     the Gentiles.

     a.   **ANSWER:** The 120 in the Upper Room
          could not receive salvation for anyone
          else nor could their receiving of the
          Spirit be automatically passed on. God
          ALWAYS deals with the individual.

2.   Tongues have ceased because "that which is
     perfect" has come - The New Testament. (Bible)

*   **1 Cor. 13:8-9**- *Charity never faileth: but
    whether there be prophecies, they shall fail;
    whether there be tongues, they shall cease;
    whether there be knowledge, it shall vanish
    away. ⁹ For we know in part, and we prophesy in
    part.*

     a.   **ANSWER:** GOD ALONE IS
          PERFECT. These verses refer to the

Christian's entrance into Glory. There will be no need for prophecies, knowledge, tongues, or any of the gifts, as Jesus will dwell with His children and speak to them face to face.

3. Tongues is the least gift.

   a. **<u>ANSWER:</u>** EVERY GIFT GOD GIVES IS IMPORTANT. In the listing of the gifts (1 Cor.12;8-10) no mention is made of which is the best. The appropriate one for the particular need is the best for the occasion. It could be that tongues and interpretation are named last as all the rest had been in operation in the Old Testament and in Christ's ministry.

In 1 Car .13: 13 Paul listed faith, hope and charity and says the latter is greatest. (Love is eternal.)

4. Tongues are only for "carnal" or "baby" Christians such as were in the Corinthian Church.

   a. **<u>ANSWER:</u>** Some at Corinth were carnal, not because they had spoken in tongues but because they were yielding to the temptations of the devil, who is always trying to lure Christians away from their steadfastness. "To be carnally minded is death," thus the warning "Grieve not the Holy Spirit." (See - whole armor of God, Eph.6:10-18)

After His baptism, Jesus was tempted of the devil for 40 days.

How BOLD is man to ACCUSE GOD of giving a gift that unnecessary and undesirable; that keeps a Christians from maturing!

5. Love is Greater.
- **1 Cor. 12:31**- *But covet earnestly the best gifts: and yet shew I unto you a more excellent way.*
  - a. **ANSWER:** Paul did not say love was greater. A more excellent hay to receive and minister the gifts was through love rather than coveting gifts. It was not a matter of having the gifts or love, but using them together.
6. Some heathen tribes speak in tongues.
  - a. **ANSWER**: The magicians of Egypt duplicated the first miracles of Moses but that did not invalidate his. The devil has great power and seeks to counterfeit everything God does. Some of his followers already have spectacular, supernatural powers that are causing amazement and wonder -unbelievable and unexplainable transportation and dematerializing of objects, etc. The day is fast approaching when "Satan with all power and signs and lying WONDERS" will deceive the WHOLE WORLD.
7. Tongues are not the only evidence.
- **Acts 2:4-** *And they were all filled with the Holy Ghost, and began to speak with other tongues, as the Spirit gave them utterance.*
  - a. **ANSWER:** It does not say had "a warm feeling;" "felt great love;" "had power;" "spoke the word with boldness:" (they

had already preached the gospel, healed the sick and cast out demons) or "a week later spoke in tongues."

Each reference to the baptism in Acts says or implies they spoke in tongues. Acts 4:31 refers to the same people who received on Pentecost. At Samaria, Simon offered money for what he saw. Peter would not have accepted an experience differing from his, as it was for this reason the Gentiles were accepted; "*As I began to speak, the Holy Ghost fell on them, AS ON US at the beginning.*" (**Acts 11:15**). "*For they heard them speak with tongues.*" (**Acts 10:46**).

8. Those who speak in tongues think they are better than Christians who don't.

   a. **ANSWER:** Two identical televisions are side by side; sound and sights are coming from one, nothing from the other. The first is not better than the other; it is being seen and heard because it is plugged into the power and turned on. "*But ye shall receive power, after that the Holy Ghost is come upon you:*" **(Acts 1:8)** "*and having received of the Father the promise of the Holy Ghost, he hath shed forth this, which ye now see and hear.*" (Acts 2:33).

9. The Baptism with the Holy Spirit with the evidence of speaking in tongues is divisive.

a. **ANSWER**: JESUS IS DIVISIVE. *"I am come to set a man at variance against his father, and the daughter against her mother, and the daughter in law against her mother in law."* (**Matt. 10:35**).

THE HOLY SPIRIT IS DIVISIVE, between those who hold to church traditions and man's interpretations of the Scriptures and those who obey Christ's "command" to be "baptized" with the Holy Spirit, yielding all - including pride and the unruly tongue: being willing to be considered *"a fool for Christ's sake."* (**1 Cor. 3:18**). The HOLY SPIRIT is also the GREAT UNIFIER. After the initial outpouring of the Holy Spirit, so great was the love for God and each other that *"them that believed were of ONE heart and ONE soul."* Gradually divisions came thru sin and disobedience; theological and cultural differences were magnified until Christ's "church," thru the centuries, has been a "broken body,'" a distorted, misrepresentation of Christianity to the world.

In this last great outpouring of the Holy Spirit, barriers are being overcome by the healing oil of the Spirit, bringing believers of all races and denominations together under the banner of LOVE, fulfilling Christ's prayer:

- **1 Pet. 2:5**- *Ye also, as lively stones, are built up a spiritual house, an holy priesthood, to offer up spiritual sacrifices, acceptable to God by Jesus Christ.*

–*Don't be in this group* –

- **Acts 7:51-52**- *Ye stiffnecked and uncircumcised in heart and ears, ye do always resist the Holy Ghost: as your fathers did, so do ye. [52] Which of the prophets have not your fathers persecuted? and they have slain them which shewed before of the coming of the Just One; of whom ye have been now the betrayers and murderers:*

10. Some new Bible versions list the last verses in Mark only as a footnote, thus imply-ing they may not be inspired.
    a. **ANSWER**: WHEN GOD REVEALED HIMSELF and His plan for the salvation of the world, He moved on holy men by the Holy Spirit to write exactly what He dic-tated, Only in the last century with the in-vention of electronic equipment has it, been possible to know the undeniable, supernatural proof that the BIBLE IS TRULY GOD'S WORD.

    FIRST and FOREMOST was the NARRATIVE - the creation of the universe, of man and His plan for both- In doing this God chose words according to their numeric value so as to form special numerical features, especially using the number 7, the very one He used in creation - 7 days in the

week, 7 colors in the spectrum, 7 notes
in music multiples of 7's for the
gestation period of hu-mans (280 days,
7x40), of animals and birds, etc.

The Bible starts with "In the beginning God
created the heavens and the earth." (28 Hebrew
letters or 7x4). Continuing on through both Old
(He-brew) and New (Greek) Testaments, every
verse contains features of sevens and multiples
of sevens.

The last verses of Mark are teeming with
numeric patterns, especially in the word
"deadly" which is mentioned only this one time
in all the New Testament but alone has 7
features of 7's!

Now the computer has revealed the most
amazing use of THE SAME WORDS but by
using equidistant spacing, the letters spelled
names of people, events and places that would
come on the world scene during the next 3.500
years, all coded in-to the structure - completely
unknown to those writing the narrative- names
such as Hitler, Anwar Sadat, Arafat, Rabin and
many others. Jesus ("YESHUA") was repeatedly
encoded throughout the Old Testament. starting
at GENESIS 1:1.

- **Isa. 46:9-10**- I am God, and there is none like
  me, declaring the end from the beginning, and
  from ancient times the things that are yet done.

No other writing in all the world has ever had
these hidden numeric features or the giving of

16

exact names and events thousands of years in advance, thus defying forgeries. Dire warnings are given to those who would add to or delete from it or preach any other gospel.

WHAT AN AWESOME GOD who created fifty billion galaxies each containing millions of billions of stars extending over a space of millions of trillions of miles yet He knows our EVERY THOUGHT. HE IS A LOVING GOD. But, *"His Spirit will not always strive with men and GREAT IS THE DAY OF HIS WRATH."* (**Rev. 6:17**). *"When ye shall SEARCH FOR ME with ALL YOU HEART I WILL BE FOUND OF YOU."* (**Jer. 29:13-14**).

BACKSLIDING

The backslider needs God's forgiveness; man's forgiveness, and forgiveness of self. (The Prodigal Son - Luke 15:11-24).

It then is a return SERIOUS to Satan OFFENSE to follow Jesus and then return to Satan's side and God does not take it lightly.

- **<u>Heb. 10:38</u>**- *Now the just shall live by faith: but if any man draw back, my soul shall have no pleasure in him.*
- **<u>Luke 9:62</u>**- *And Jesus said unto him, No man, having put his hand to the plough, and looking back, is fit for the kingdom of God.*

God's great mercy always allows a "space for repentance," (Cain, King Saul, Jezebel- spoken of in Rev.2:20-21, etc.) Although King David com-mitted terrible sins - adultery and murder, he truly repented and confessed to God or he would have been subject to His law: "*No adulterer or murderer shall inherit the kingdom of God.*" (**Gal. 5:19-21**). Judas repented and confessed, but to men instead of God. (Matt. 27:3-5).

- **Isa. 55:7**- *Let the wicked forsake his way, and the unrighteous man his thoughts: and let him return unto the LORD, and he will have mercy upon him; and to our God, for he will abundantly pardon.*
- **Heb. 7:25**- *Wherefore he is able also to save them to the uttermost that come unto God by him, seeing he ever liveth to make intercession for them.*

- **2 Pet. 3:9**- *The Lord is not slack concerning his promise, as some men count slackness; but is longsuffering to us-ward, not willing that any should perish, but that all should come to repentance.*
- **2 Chron. 7:14**- *If my people, which are called by my name, shall humble themselves, and pray, and seek my face, and turn from their wicked ways; then will I hear from heaven, and will forgive their sin, and will heal their land.*
- **Jer. 3:22**- *Return, ye backsliding children, and I will heal your backslidings. Behold, we come unto thee; for thou art the LORD our God.*

If you have turned away from Jesus, right now pray this prayer of confession, or one similar. God forgave David and He will forgive you if you pray with all sincerity of heart.

"Oh GOD, have mercy upon me. I acknowledge and repent of my transgressions, for it was against Thee that I sinned. I am truly sorry that I brought shame upon the name of Thy Son and I claim His blood for the cleansing of my iniqui-ty. Make me to know peace, joy and gladness a-gain. Create in me a clean heart and renew a right spirit within me. Forgive me for causing others to suffer. Help me to be an overcomer - never again to follow the enticements of the devil. I sincerely want to be Thy child, AMEN. (Read all of Psalms 51).

- **Hos. 14:4**- *I will heal their backsliding, I will love them freely: for mine anger is turned away from him.*

- **Phil. 3:13-14**- *Brethren, I count not myself to have apprehended: but this one thing I do, forgetting those things which are behind, and reaching forth unto those things which are before, [14] I press toward the mark for the prize of the high calling of God in Christ Jesus.*

- **John 8:11-** *She said, No man, Lord. And Jesus said unto her, Neither do I condemn thee: go, and sin no more.*

- **Prov. 29:1**- *He, that being often reproved hardeneth his neck, shall suddenly be destroyed, and that without remedy.*

*****

The main causes for backsliding are:

- Lack of spiritual insight and true commitment
- Neglect of daily Bible reading, prayer and fellowship with other believers
- Love of money and worldly pleasures
- Corruption from evil companions

- **2 Pet. 2:20**- *For if after they have escaped the pollutions of the world through the knowledge of the Lord and Saviour Jesus Christ, they are again entangled therein, and overcome, the latter end is worse with them than the beginning.*

<u>COMFORT</u>

- **<u>Heb. 13:5</u>-** *Let your conversation be without covetousness; and be content with such things as ye have: for he hath said, I will never leave thee, nor forsake thee.*
- **<u>Psa. 27:10</u>-** *When my father and my mother forsake me, then the LORD will take me up.*
- **<u>Matt. 11:28</u>-** *Come unto me, all ye that labour and are heavy laden, and I will give you rest.*
- **2 Cor. 1:3-4-** *Blessed be God, even the Father of our Lord Jesus Christ, the Father of mercies, and the God of all comfort; 4 Who comforteth us in all our tribulation, that we may be able to comfort them which are in any trouble, by the comfort wherewith we ourselves are comforted of God.*
- **<u>Psa. 119:49-50</u>-** *Remember the word unto thy servant, upon which thou hast caused me to hope. 50 This is my comfort in my affliction: for thy word hath quickened me.*
- **<u>Isa. 61:1</u>-** *The Spirit of the Lord GOD is upon me; because the LORD hath anointed me to*

preach good tidings unto the meek; he hath sent me to bind up the brokenhearted, to proclaim liberty to the captives, and the opening of the prison to them that are bound;

- **John 14:16-** *And I will pray the Father, and he shall give you another Comforter, that he may abide with you forever; (See "Holy Spirit")*

Loss of a Loved One

- **1 Thess. 4:13-** *But I would not have you to be ignorant, brethren, concerning them which are asleep, that ye sorrow not, even as others which have no hope.*

- **2 Cor. 5:6-8-** *Therefore we are always confident, knowing that, whilst we are at home in the body, we are absent from the Lord: [7] (For we walk by faith, not by sight:) [8] We are confident, I say, and willing rather to be absent from the body, and to be present with the Lord.*

- **Rev. 21:4-** *And God shall wipe away all tears from their eyes; and there shall be no more death, neither sorrow, nor crying, neither shall there be any more pain: for the former things are passed away.*

- **Psa. 23:4-** *Yea, though I walk through the valley of the shadow of death, I will fear no evil: for thou art with me; thy rod and thy staff they comfort me.*

- **Matt. 5:4-** *Blessed are they that mourn: for they shall be comforted.*

COVENANTS

A COVENANT is an agreement between two or more parties, either verbal or in writing. Usually a token is given or exchanged.

The FIRST COVENANT between GOD and MAN was in the Garden of Eden; the shedding of BLOOD (the death) of an animal would be accepted by God as a substitute covering for sin.

With Abraham and his descendants God made a cove-nant to give them the land of Canaan (present-day Israel) as an everlasting possession and He would be their God. The token was circumcision, BLOOD shed on man's part (Gen.17:718).

When Moses led the Children of Israel (Abraham's descendants) out of Egypt to the Promised Land, God made a covenant, again with the blood of an animal and the giving of the law, His Ten Commandments, as the tokens. This covenant they broke (Heb.8:9). Fifteen hundred years later God made a NEW COVENANT not only with the Jews but with all mankind of an eternal inheritance and the token was the BLOOD of HIS OWN SON. (Heb. 9:14-15) .

Amazingly, the VERY FIRST COVENANT God established was between man and woman, that of MARRIAGE, which was also sealed by the shedding of BLOOD on the wedding night. This was a lifelong commitment of FIDELITY by BOTH PARTIES.

Since the Garden of Eden, Satan has tempted men and women to break God's covenants. The JEWS broke His commandments and for 2,700 years became wanderers-suffering as no other people.

In these end days, Satan is waging a full-scale war. Because of suggestive television, pornography, child molestation, incest, homosexuals, etc. virginity of both parties is a rarity so that a TRUE MARRIAGE COVENANT can be establish-ed. He has made illicit sex", "affairs" and divorce so commonplace that FEW marriages can survive his onslaught. God is a God of love but also of WRATH and He is now letting the world rea the CONSEQUENCES of breaking this FIRST of all blood covenants: divorce, abortion (murder), violence, venereal diseases, and AIDS, against

which MAN is HELPLESS and that not only
THREATENS everyone's lifestyle but our very
EXISTENCE!

Children and young people should be taught the fear of
the Lord and as soon as possible to enter into the blood
covenant of salvation and to keep themselves PURE to
enter 1nto the SACRED MARRIAGE COVENANT at
the PROPER TIME and receive God's blessings and
protection. YOUNG PEOPLE, don't let SATAN TRAP
YOU! Learn to say, "NO."

CULTS/ OCCULT

Satan is the instigator of all opposition to God and is the power behind all cults and the occult. He is not a figment of the imagination; the butt of jokes; characterized as a red- suited, pitchfork-wielding, horned individual; the opposite is the truth. His original abode was heaven, with "top" position of "Covering Cherub," "perfect in his ways with great wisdom and brightness" and "with every precious stones as his covering." (Ezek. 28:13).

Pride entered into him: "I will exalt my throne above the stars of God. I will be like the most High" and he became "filled with violence." Then God decreed: "Thine heart was lifted up because of thy beauty. Thou hast corrupted thy wisdom, thou hast sinned. I will destroy thee." (Ezek. 28: 16).

God will never again allow a rebellion in heaven, so before anyone is allowed entrance, true love and unshakeable allegiance to God must be proven. Thus He did not create man as a robot but instead with the irrevocable gift of free will of choice, not forcing anyone to love Him.

Therefore, Satan was allowed to retain tremen-dous wisdom and power, along with the violence he acquired, and given this earth as a temporary domain to try the souls of men. He is likened to "a roaring lion" that goes about "seeking whom he may devour." (1 Pet. 5:8) He truly has the nature of a vicious, heartless animal but he "transforms" himself "into an angel of light." He is the source of all evil , lawlessness, lies, and lying wonders and his retinue of demons assist by oppressing and possessing victims who will let them in; impersonating the dead to promote reincarnation and spiritualism.

Satan relentlessly attacks the Bible for it reveals who he is; exposes his tactics and pronounces his doom of eternal punishment along with all those who follow him.

He proclaims evolution and atheism so, as an animal, man does not have to curb his lustful nature nor feel the condemnation of having to answer for it to a holy God.

For these thousands of years he has constantly created new religions and cults with their false teachers and false prophets to keep people in spiritual darkness and bondage.

- **2 Cor. 4:4**- *In whom the god of this world hath blinded the minds of them which believe not, lest the light of the glorious gospel of Christ, who is the image of God, should shine unto them.*
- **John 14:6**- *Jesus saith unto him, I am the way, the truth, and the life: no man cometh unto the Father, but by me.*

- **Deut. 18:10-12**- *There shall not be found among you any one that maketh his son or his daughter to pass through the fire, or that useth divination* **(fortune telling, Ouija boards, automatic writing),** *or an observer of times* **(a person who deals with astrology and horoscopes),** *or an enchanter* **(magician),** *or a witch* **(one making compacts with evil spirits-thus possessing supernatural powers).** [11] *Or a charmer (hypnotist), or a consulter with familiar spirits* **(Spiritist medium)**, *or a wizard* **(clairvoyant, psychic, ESP, telepathy),** *or a necromancer* **(one who supposedly communicates with the dead; séances; voodoo)**. [12] *For all that do these things are an abomination unto the* LORD: *and because of these abominations the* LORD *thy God doth drive them out from before thee.*

Yoga; Transcendental Meditation; Sun Moon's Unification Church; The Way, The Truth and the Life; The Way; The Children of God; Satanism, etc. ALL DENY that JESUS is GOD.

- **Isa. 9:8**- *... and his name shall be called Wonderful, Counsellor, The mighty God, The everlasting Father, The Prince of Peace.*
- **Heb. 9:27**- *And as it is appointed unto men once to die, but after this the judgment:*
- **Luke 16:22-23**- *And it came to pass, that the beggar died, and was carried by the angels into Abraham's bosom: the rich man also died, and was buried;* [23] *And in hell he lift up his eyes, being in torments...*
- **Matt. 24:5, 24**- *For many shall come in my name, saying, I am Christ; and shall deceive many.* [24] *For there shall arise false Christs, and*

false prophets, and shall shew great signs and wonders; insomuch that, if it were possible, they shall deceive the very elect.

Your ultimate future is controlled by YOUR DECISION ALONE; not in cards, nor the stars, "Choose you this day whom you will serve." (Jos. 24:15).

Jesus said: I AM THE DO0R, by me if any man enter in he shall be saved. Come into me… and I will give you rest. (John 10:9).

DEAR JESUS, I do come to You; I want Your rest. I have been searching for the truth and I did not realize I was being led astray by the dev-il. I now RESIST him; RENOUNCE him; and want no part with him here or hereafter. Jesus, I am sorry I sinned; I accept You as my Savior . I claim Your blood as the atonement for all my sins. Help me to clearly recognize what is of You and what is of Satan. I believe You have heard this prayer and have freed -me from his power. Thank You for saving me. From this day on help me to bring honor to Your name. AMEN.

- **Phil. 4:13**- *I can do all things through Christ which strengtheneth me.*
- **2 Cor. 6:17**- *Wherefore come out from among them, and be ye separate, saith the Lord, and touch not the unclean thing; and I will receive you.*
- **Eph. 6:17**- *…be strong in the Lord, and in the power of his might. [11] Put on the whole armour of God, that ye may be able to stand against the wiles of the devil. [12] For we wrestle not against flesh and blood, but against principalities, against powers, against the rulers of the*

darkness of this world, against spiritual wickedness in high places. [13] Wherefore take unto you the whole armour of God, that ye may be able to withstand in the evil day, and having done all, to stand. [14] Stand therefore, having your loins girt about with truth, and having on the breastplate of righteousness; [15] And your feet shod with the preparation of the gospel of peace; [16] Above all, taking the shield of faith, wherewith ye shall be able to quench all the fiery darts of the wicked. [17] And take the helmet of salvation, and the sword of the Spirit, which is the word of God: [18] Praying always with all prayer and supplication in the Spirit, and watching thereunto with all perseverance and supplication for all saints; (See "Holy Spirit")

- **Rev. 12:11**- *And they overcame him by the blood of the Lamb, and by the word of their testimony;*

The devil is the great imitator of God. He appears as "an angel of light" but his "miracles" glorify himself, not God, and are SPECTACULAR, not beneficial. His apparent blessings turn into cursings and tragedies.

He imitates all the gifts of the Holy Spirit; gives advice, reveals mysteries (such as names, numbers, where to find lost articles, etc.) ; gives supernatural faith (to walk barefooted over hot coals, to be transported from one place to another); gives power to perform miracles (such as dematerializing articles, bending metal, etc.) ; predict the future, etc.

Yoga and Transcendental Meditation are part of the Hindu religion. One needs only to see photographs of that country or to visit it to know that the religions of

India have done nothing for it but keep millions of people in superstition, extreme poverty, and demonic bondage. The principle teaching is that the soul is imprisoned in the body and must be liberated after many reincarnations. The physical exercises and men-tal disciplines are designed to overcome the body of flesh and each position is a form of prayer. It is impossible that the repetition of a Word given by an unbeliever before a pagan altar is acceptable to God. Jesus said, "When you. Pray use not vain repetitions, as the heathen do." David prayed, "Let the words of my mouth and the meditations of my heart be acceptable in Thy sight, O Lord... Blessed is the man that walks not in the counsel of the ungodly." (Psa.

Astrology is condemned in the Bible as "an abomination." (Deut. 18). It is a pagan practice which encourages people to consult the powers of darkness instead of God. It is fatalistic, tending to paralyze initiative and right judgment and excuses man from his responsibility before God.

His word says: "In all your ways acknowledge Him and HE shall direct your paths. Delight your also in the Lord, and He shall give you the desires of your heart. The steps of a righteous man are ordered of the Lord, and He delights in his way."

The works of the devil DESTROY PEACE and HAPPINESS, and plant seeds of discord and fear, but Isaiah wrote of the manifestations of the Holy Spirit, "This is the rest... and this is the refreshing."

<u>DEATH- LIFE AFTER DEATH</u>

- **<u>James 4:14</u>**- *...For what is your life? It is even a vapor, that appeareth for a little time, and then vanisheth away.*
- **<u>Job 14:14</u>**- *If a man die, shall he live again? all the days of my appointed time will I wait, till my change come.*

These questions have plagued men and wo-men through the ages.

GOD is the AUTHOR of both LIFE and DEATH; therefore, His word is the ONLY true and final AUTHORITY on both. (See "<u>Word of God</u>" and "<u>You Shall Know, the Truth.</u>")

- **<u>Gen. 2:7</u>**- *The LORD God formed man of the dust of the ground, and breathed into his nostrils the breath of life; and man became a living soul.*
- **<u>Gen. 2:17</u>**- *But of the tree of the knowledge of good and evil, thou shalt not eat of it: for in the*

*day that thou eatest thereof thou shalt surely
DIE.*

Any thought, word, action, omission, or desire, contrary
to the law of God is SIN.

- **Ezek. 18:4**- *...The soul that sinneth, it shall
  DIE. And without the shedding of blood is no
  remission (of sin) (Heb. 9:22).*

These laws of God are just as true and lasting as His <u>law
of gravity</u>, etc.

- **Rom. 5:12**- *Wherefore, as by one man (Adam)
  sin entered into the world, and death by sin; and
  so DEATH passed upon ALL men, for that ALL
  HAVE SINNED:*

Adam and Eve, in fear and shame, hid them-selves from
the presence of the Lord after disobeying Him. From that
day to this, their descendants (<u>all</u> people <u>everywhere</u>),
having inherited their fallen nature, fear giving an
account for sinful thoughts and actions to a holy God.
They may not have read His law: "It is appointed unto
man ONCE to die, and after this the judgment:"
{Heb.9:27) yet in their innermost being there is a
consciousness of accountability to a Supreme Being.

The archaeological findings around the world show a
universal belief in a life after death but without the
assurance of divine forgiveness, man FEARS his
APPOINTMENT with GOD.

- **1 Cor. 15:56-** *The sting of death is sin; and the
  strength of sin is the law.*

- **Ezek. 33:11-** *Say unto them, As I live, saith the Lord GOD, I have no pleasure in the death of the wicked; but that the wicked turn from his way and live: turn ye, turn ye from your evil ways; for why will ye die, O house of Israel?*

- **1 Cor. 15:21, 22, 54, 57-** *For since by man came death, by man came also the resurrection of the dead. [22] For as in Adam all die, even so in Christ shall all be made alive. [54] So when this corruptible shall have put on incorruption, and this mortal shall have put on immortality, then shall be brought to pass the saying that is written, Death is swallowed up in victory. [55] O death, where is thy sting? O grave, where is thy victory? [56] The sting of death is sin; and the strength of sin is the law. [57] But thanks be to God, which giveth us the victory through our Lord Jesus Christ.*

- **John 11:25-26-** *Jesus said unto her, I am the resurrection, and the life: he that believeth in me, though he were dead, yet shall he live: [26] And whosoever liveth and believeth in me shall never die. Believest thou this?*

- **2 Cor. 5:1, 6, 8-** *For we know that if our earthly house of this tabernacle were dissolved, we have a building of God, an house not made with hands, eternal in the heavens. [6] Therefore we are always confident, knowing that, whilst we are at home in the body, we are absent from the Lord: [8] We are confident, I say, and willing rather to be absent from the body, and to be present with the Lord.*

Therefore, death for the true believer is a separation of the soul from the earthly body to go to be present with the Lord, while his body sleeps (remains in the grave. At the coming of Jesus to catch out the "church," the souls of the "dead in Christ" coming with Him will be reunited with their glorified, spiritual bodies--as a butterfly from a cocoon, as a new plant from a dead seed. It will be raised in incorruption, in glory, in power, bearing the image of the heavenly and be immortal; never to know sorrow, crying, pain or death. (Rev. 21:1-4). However, the individual's identity will not be lost.

- **1 Cor. 13:12**- *For now we see through a glass, darkly; but then face to face: now I know in part; but then shall I know even as also I am known.*

Is it any wonder the Christian is admonished to overcome? (Rev.2-3).

- **1 Cor. 15:58**- *Therefore, my beloved brethren, be ye stedfast, unmoveable, always abounding in the work of the Lord, forasmuch as ye know that your labour is not in vain in the Lord.*
- **Psa. 23:4**- *Yea, though I walk through the valley of the shadow of death, I will fear no evil: for thou art with me; thy rod and thy staff they comfort me.*

Much is being said and written at this time about deathbed experiences: the spirit floating out of the physical body, encountering a brilliant white light, seeing into heaven, encountering dead loved ones, feeling wonderful joy and peace. Some see a review of their entire life with the realization that there is no possibility of lying or concealing anything. Most report that the beauty is indescribable.

All these should cause the "unsaved" to prepare to die--
which is the reason God gave most of the experiences--
as the believer already <u>knows</u> he has <u>eternal life</u>.

Satan, knowing his time is short, is seizing upon the
opportunity to deceive the world, still using DEATH as
the <u>bait</u> in his trap as he did with Eve: "*Ye shall <u>not</u>
surely <u>die</u>.*" He has jumped on the band wagon and is
helping with the campaign to rid people of their fear of
death. He plays up "life after life" but twists or slants the
accounts so that it would seem there is not always
judgment before God; that sinful deeds are looked upon
only with "understanding" and even with humor.

As with nearly all reporting on any subject- especially
political and religious---the conclusion to the matter, or
the impression left, depends upon the background and
convictions of the reporter---although the inferences may
be unintentional.

JESUS, who came down from heaven, lived upon this
earth, died, descended into hell, arose and ascended into
heaven; who is the way, the truth and the life, SAID that
"life after life" for those who believed on him, would be
beyond human comprehension.

- **1 Cor. 2:9**- *But as it is written, Eye hath not
  seen, nor ear heard, neither have entered into
  the heart of man, the things which God hath
  prepared for them that love him.*

Jesus also told of the condition of those who die, having
not accepted him.

- **John 3:36**- *He that believeth on the Son hath
  everlasting life: and he that believeth not the*

Son shall not see life; but the wrath of God abideth on him.

- **Matt. 25:30-** *And cast ye the unprofitable servant into outer darkness: there shall be weeping and gnashing of teeth.*

Jesus told of the rich man who "died, was buried; and in hell he lift up his eyes, being in torments…"

A Tibetan Book of the Dead is being referred to which contains similar 'out of body' experiences that were handed down for generations by word of mouth before being written down. The devil very subtly causes people to draw the conclusion that if followers of non-Christian religions have had similar experiences, then Jesus is not the only way to heaven--thus making Him a liar. "No man cometh to the Father but by Me." (John 14:6).

- **Isa. 45:22-** *Look unto me, and be ye saved, all the ends of the earth: for I am God, and there is none else.*

If all the original details and background circumstances were known, it would undoubtedly be found that God was dealing supernaturally to show the true way to Him for all are descendants of Noah--- whom He saved from the Flood--- as were Socrates and Plato, accounting for their belief of life after death. Enoch, the 7th from Adam, was translated that he did not see (experience) death but he testified to believing in the Lord and His return.

- **Jude 1:14-15-** *Behold, the Lord cometh with ten thousands of his saints, [15] To execute judgment upon all… (Rev.   19:11-21; 20:4).*

Job, a contemporary of Abraham (1520 B. C.) declared:

- **Job 19:25-27**- *For I know that my redeemer liveth, and that he shall stand at the latter day upon the earth: [26] And though after my skin worms destroy this body, yet in my flesh shall I see God: [27] Whom I shall see for myself, and mine eyes shall behold, and not another; though my reins be consumed within me.*
- **2 Cor. 5:10**- *For we must all appear before the judgment seat of Christ; that every one may receive the things done in his body, according to that he hath done, whether it be good or bad.*
- **Rev. 20:15**- *And whosoever was not found written in the book of life was cast into the lake of fire.*

*The **LOST** will have an eternal body for there will be **EVERLASTING PUNISHMENT**. (Matt. 25: 46).*

They will have feeling, sight, hearing, mem-ory, concern for others, (Luke 16:19-31) But, NO HOPE!

- **Prov. 11:7**- *When a wicked man dieth, his expectation shall perish: and the hope of unjust men perisheth.*

Everyone lives on hope. No matter how terrible the circumstances, "while there is life there is hope" but how UNIMAGINABLY HORRIBLE to NEVER again have HOPE for a change, to see a ray of sunlight, to hear a kindly word, to feel a tinder touch, or to take a cooling sip of water, or be free from PAIN and REGRET.

Don't put off another minute preparing to die! "Seek the. Lord, and ye shall LIVE." (Life after life in eternal bliss!).

- **Rom. 6:23**- *For the wages of sin is death; but the gift of God is eternal life through Jesus Christ our Lord.*

(Suggested Prayer)

DEAR GOD. I am a sinner and need Thy forgiveness. I repent of my every thought, word and deed that has been wrong in Thy sight. I renounce the devil and all known sins. I believe that Christ died for me, and that He arose from the dead and is now at Thy right hand. Jesus, I accept Thee as my Savior and Lord of my life. Lead me by Thy Holy Spirit that I may know Thy will in all things. I thank Thee for saving me. Amen. (See "Holy Spirit" and "Second Coming")

****

The "saved" dead are with the Lord. (2 Cor. 5:8) They, along with the 'raptured' believers, will stand before the judgment seat of Christ for their works but not their sins. (2 Cor. 5:10; 1 Cor. 3:10-15). They will rule and reign with Him on this earth for a thousand years of peace. (Rev. 20:4; Isa. 11:4-9) They will not be tempted when Satan is "loosed for a short season," nor will they marry or reproduce. They are as the angels. (Matt. 22:30) They will not be in the great white throne judgment but will dwell in the New Jerusalem with God Himself and the Lamb (Jesus) forever.

The "ungodly" - from Adam on - go immediately at death to Hades (sheol, hell) where they are tormented. (Luke 16:19-31).

After the Millennium and "short season," they will be resurrected and appear at the great white throne judgment. They will acknowledge Jesus as Lord before the Father but it will be too late to acknowledge Him as their Savior.

- **Phil. 2:10**- *That at the name of Jesus every knee should bow, of things in heaven, and things in earth, and things under the earth;*

They will be judged according to their works and then cast into the lake of fire to be tormented day and night forever and ever. (Rev.20: 15; Mat. 8:12; 22:13)

No one should interfere with the "appointment" God has planned for each person. He alone knows when and how He wants you to leave this life and enter into His presence. Don't let anything or anybody influence you to decide your time of exit (suicide) or anyone else's (murder). Even though at times you may not believe it, <u>GOD ALWAYS KNOWS BEST.</u>

DISCOURAGEMENT

The Bible warns us we must stand *"against the wiles of the devil and the fiery darts of the wicked."* (**Eph. 6:11-16**). DISCOURAGEMENT is one of the main darts and is aimed at every one of God's children.

- **1 Pet. 5:8**- *Be sober, be vigilant; because your adversary the devil, as a roaring lion, walketh about, seeking whom he may devour:*
- **James 4:7-8**- *Submit yourselves therefore to God. Resist the devil, and he will flee from you. ⁸ Draw nigh to God, and he will draw nigh to you. Cleanse your hands, ye sinners; and purify your hearts, ye double minded.*
- **Jos. 1:9**- *Have not I commanded thee? Be strong and of a good courage; be not afraid, neither be thou dismayed: for the LORD thy God is with thee whithersoever thou goest.*

- **Psa. 42:11**- *Why art thou cast down, O my soul? and why art thou disquieted within me? hope thou in God: for I shall yet praise him, who is the health of my countenance, and my God.*

- **Hebrews 10:23**- *Let us hold fast the profession of our faith without wavering; (for he is faithful that promised;)*

- **1 Pet. 5:7**- *Casting all your care upon him; for he careth for you.*

- **Psa. 55:22**- *Cast thy burden upon the LORD, and he shall sustain thee: he shall never suffer the righteous to be moved.*

- **Heb. 10:35-36**- *Cast not away therefore your confidence, which hath great recompence of reward. [36] For ye have need of patience, that, after ye have done the will of God, ye might receive the promise.*

- **Psa. 37:4-5**- *Delight thyself also in the LORD: and he shall give thee the desires of thine heart. [5] Commit thy way unto the LORD; trust also in him; and he shall bring it to pass.*

Acts 14:22- *Confirming the souls of the disciples, and exhorting them to continue in the faith, and that we must through much tribulation enter into the kingdom of God.*

- **Heb. 12:1-3**- Wherefore seeing we also are compassed about with so great a cloud of witnesses, let us lay aside every weight, and the sin which doth so easily beset us, and let us run with patience the race that is set before us, [2] Looking unto Jesus the author and finisher of our faith; who for the joy that was set before him endured the cross, despising the shame, and is set down at the right hand of the throne of God. [3] For consider him that endured such contradiction of sinners against himself, lest ye be wearied and faint in your minds.

- **1 Cor. 9:24**- *Know ye not that they which run in a race run all, but one receiveth the prize? So run, that ye may obtain.*

- **Deut. 1:21**- *Behold, the LORD thy God hath set the land before thee: go up and possess it, as the LORD God of thy fathers hath said unto thee; fear not, neither be discouraged.*

- **Heb. 3:13-14**- *But exhort one another daily, while it is called To day; lest any of you be hardened through the deceitfulness of sin. [14] For we are made partakers of Christ, if we hold the beginning of our confidence steadfast unto the end;*

- **Heb. 13:20-21**- *Now the God of peace, that brought again from the dead our Lord Jesus, that great shepherd of the sheep, through the blood of the everlasting covenant, [21] Make you perfect in every good work to do his will, working in you that which is well pleasing in his sight, through Jesus Christ; to whom be glory for ever and ever. Amen.*

DRUGS

God made man in His own image, FORMING THE
human body to be the temple for the Spirit of God to
dwell in. He gave man the most precious OF GIFTS –
THE MIND, Which is perhaps one -if not the greatest-of
His masterpieces. As marvelous and intricate as the
computer is, it is only copied after man's brain; which is
humanly impossible to exactly duplicate.
The mind is TO BE USED PRIMARILY TO LEARN
About God and HIS REQUIREMENTS FOR
ETERNAL life, along WITH LIVING HAPPILY IN
THIS present world. Satan, as man's arch enemy, is
therefore determined TO DEBILITATE AND eventually
completely CAPTIVATE THE MIND; rendering his
victim mentally incapable of obeying God's laws on this
earth and obtaining eternal life in heaven.

ALL DRUGS - marijuana, LSD, acid, speed, cocaine,
heroin, alcohol, tobacco – are TOOLS OF SATAN and
to take them is to sin AGAINST God. Each OF These
evils lead to bondage, destruction and damnation. Drugs
are being decriminalized; enslaving destructive effects
denied but god says: "woe unto them who call evil

good."

- **Rom. 6:23**- *For the wages of sin is death; but the gift of God is eternal life through Jesus Christ our Lord.*
- **Prov. 11:19**- *As righteousness tendeth to life: so he that pursueth evil pursueth it to his own death.*
- **1 Cor. 3:16-17**- *Know ye not that ye are the temple of God, and that the Spirit of God dwelleth in you? [17] If any man defile the temple of God, him shall God destroy; for the temple of God is holy, which temple ye are.*

But YOU CAN BE DELIVERED from the captivity of Satan, lust, and drugs.

- **Luke 4:18**- *The Spirit of the Lord is upon me, because he hath anointed me to preach the gospel to the poor; he hath sent me to heal the brokenhearted, to preach deliverance to the captives, and recovering of sight to the blind, to set at liberty them that are bruised,*
- **Titus 3:3-5**- *For we ourselves also were sometimes foolish, disobedient, deceived, serving divers lusts and pleasures, living in malice and envy, hateful, and hating one another. [4] But after that the kindness and love of God our Saviour toward man appeared, [5] Not by works of righteousness which we have done, but according to his mercy he saved us, by the washing of regeneration, and renewing of the*

Holy Ghost;

- **Acts 3:19**- *Repent ye therefore, and be converted, that your sins may be blotted out, when the times of refreshing shall come from the presence of the Lord.*
- **Isa. 1:18**- *Come now, and let us reason together, saith the LORD: though your sins be as scarlet, they shall be as white as snow; though they be red like crimson, they shall be as wool.*
- **Rom. 10:13**- *For whosoever shall call upon the name of the Lord shall be saved.*
- **1 John 1:9**- *If we confess our sins, he is faithful and just to forgive us our sins, and to cleanse us from all unrighteousness.*
- **2 Cor. 5:17**- *Therefore if any man be in Christ, he is a new creature: old things are passed away; behold, all things are become new.*
- **John 8:36**- *If the Son therefore shall make you free, ye shall be free indeed.*
- **Romans 12:1-2**- *I beseech you therefore, brethren, by the mercies of God, that ye present your bodies a living sacrifice, holy, acceptable unto God, which is your reasonable service. [2] And be not conformed to this world: but be ye transformed by the renewing of your mind, that ye may prove what is that good, and acceptable, and perfect, will of God.*
- **James 4:7**- *Submit yourselves therefore to God. Resist the devil, and he will flee from you.*
- **Romans 13:14**- *But put ye on the Lord Jesus Christ, and make not provision for the flesh, to*

fulfil the lusts thereof.

Destroy everything you have that is of Satan; buy no more; accept no more. If you want God to mean business with you, you must mean busi-ness with Him. Determine that Satan will nev-er again rob you of your senses and that you will "bring into captivity every thought to the obedience of Christ."

- **1 Cor. 6:20**- *For ye are bought with a price: therefore glorify God in your body, and in your spirit, which are God's.*
- **Col. 3:17**- *And whatsoever ye do in word or deed, do all in the name of the Lord Jesus, giving thanks to God and the Father by him.*

(See also "Thoughts" and "Holy Spirit")

ETERNAL SAFETY

Jesus is "not willing that any should perish," but all will not be saved, ONLY those who repent and "receive Him." Therefore, salvation involves the "TWO." "No man" (THIRD PARTY) can take a person out of God's hand. Yet God never takes away the individual's freedom of choice, He FORCES NO ONE to accept Him nor to stay with Him.

He does not have a double standard -- one for "under the law" and another for "under grace," for all are saved by faith, either looking forward to the coming of the Savior or looking back to it. No one ever kept the law and Abraham, Isaac, Jacob, Joseph, etc. had no law.

God is no respecter of persons.

- **Heb. 13:8**- *Jesus Christ the same yesterday, and today, and forever.*
- **Heb. 3:12-14**- *Take heed, brethren, lest there be in any of you an evil heart of unbelief, in departing from the living God. [13] But exhort one*

another daily, while it is called Today; lest any of you be hardened through the deceitfulness of sin. *14 For we are made partakers of Christ, if we hold the beginning of our confidence steadfast unto the end;*

- **Heb. 2:1-3-** *Therefore we ought to give the more earnest heed to the things which we have heard, lest at any time we should let them slip. 2 For if the word spoken by angels was steadfast, and every transgression and disobedience received a just recompense of reward; 3 How shall we escape, if we neglect so great salvation; which at the first began to be spoken by the Lord, and was confirmed unto us by them that heard him;*

- **Matt. 24:13**- *But he that shall endure unto the end, the same shall be saved.*

- **Heb. 6:5-6**- *And have tasted the good word of God, and the powers of the world to come, 6 If they shall fall away, to renew them again unto repentance; seeing they crucify to themselves the Son of God afresh, and put him to an open shame.*

- **Col. 1:23**- *If ye continue in the faith grounded and settled, and be not moved away from the hope of the gospel, which ye have heard, and which was preached to every creature which is under heaven; whereof I Paul am made a minister;*

- **Heb. 10:23, 26-27, 29**- *23 Let us hold fast the profession of our faith without wavering; (for he is faithful that promised;) 26 For if we sin willfully after that we have received the* knowledge of the truth, there remaineth no more sacrifice for sins, *27 But a certain fearful looking for of judgment and fiery indignation, which shall devour the adversaries. 29 Of how much sorer punishment, suppose ye, shall he be thought worthy, who hath trodden underfoot the Son of God, and hath counted the blood of the covenant, wherewith he was sanctified, an unholy thing, and hath done despite unto the Spirit of grace?*

- **2 Pet. 2:20-22**- *For if after they have escaped the pollutions of the world through the knowledge of the Lord and Savior Jesus Christ, they are again entangled therein, and overcome, the latter end is worse with them than the beginning. 21 For it had been better for them not to have known the way of righteousness, than, after they have known it, to turn from the holy commandment delivered unto them. 22 But it is happened unto them according to the true proverb, The dog is turned to his own vomit again; and the sow that was washed to her wallowing in the mire.*

- **Rom. 11:21-22**- *For if God spared not the natural branches, take heed lest he also spare not thee. 22 Behold therefore the goodness and severity of God: on them which fell, severity; but toward thee, goodness, if thou continue in his goodness: otherwise thou also shalt be cut off.*

- **Ex. 32:33**- *And the LORD said unto Moses, Whosoever hath sinned against me, him will I blot out of my book.*

- **Rev. 3:5**- *He that overcometh, the same shall be clothed in white raiment; and I will not blot out his name out of the book of life, but I will* *confess his name before my Father, and before his angels.*

- **1 Sam. 10:6**- *And the Spirit of the LORD will come upon thee, and thou shalt prophesy with them, and shalt be turned into another man.*

- **1 Sam. 15:10**- *The word of the Lord came unto Samuel (concerning Saul) he is turned back from following me.*

- **1 Sam. 28:16-** *Then, said Samuel (to Saul) wherefore then dost thou ask of me seeing the Lord is departed from thee, and is become thine enemy.*

- **1 Chron. 28:2,9**- *Then David the king stood up upon his feet, and said, Hear me, my brethren, and my people: As for me, I had in mine heart to build an house of rest for the ark of the covenant of the LORD, and for the footstool of our God, and had made ready for the building: [9] And thou, Solomon my son, know thou the God of thy father, and serve him with a perfect heart and with a willing mind: for the LORD searcheth all hearts, and understandeth all the imaginations of the thoughts: if thou seek him, he will be found of thee; but if thou forsake him, he will cast thee off forever.*

- **1 Kings 11:9**- *And the LORD was angry with Solomon, because his heart was turned from the LORD God of Israel, which had appeared unto him twice,*

- **Ezek. 3:20**- *Again, When a righteous man doth turn from his righteousness, and commit iniquity, and I lay a stumblingblock before him, he shall die: because thou hast not given him warning, he shall die in his sin, and his righteousness which he hath done shall not be* *remembered; but his blood will I require at thine hand.*

- **2 Pet. 3:17-18**- *Ye therefore, beloved, seeing ye know these things before, beware lest ye also, being led away with the error of the wicked, fall from your own steadfastness. [18] But grow in grace, and in the knowledge of our Lord and Savior Jesus Christ. To him be glory both now and for ever. Amen.*
- **2 Pet. 1:10-** *Wherefore the rather, brethren, give diligence to make your calling and election sure: for if ye do these things, ye shall never fall:*

To be shocked, badly burned or killed is not electricity's fault but rather the individual's for not complying with its laws. The same applies to God's laws.

If you are depending up God "excusing" the sins of "Christians" and He doesn't, you have lost ALL. Repent now and start walking even AS HE WALKED." Be SAFE not SORRY!

In spite of absolute evidence of unbelievable evil and demonic activity all around, few people really believe there is a devil and a burning hell.

Through the ages Satan's (Lucifer) great desire has been to be worshipped as God and to rule over this earth. Many times he has almost achieved the latter and God will allow him to do so for 7 years prior to the return of Jesus to reign for 1,000 years of peace. (Rev. 20:4).

Knowing his time is short, Satan is truly "as a roaring lion seeking whom he may DEVOUR whom RESIST steadfast in the faith." (**1 Pet. 5:8-9**).

His prime aim is to destroy the Bible (not only by open ridicule and falsehoods but by "new" translations); to defame the name and person of Jesus; to replace God with "the Force"; to silence Christians and suppress their activities through intimidation and false accusations or by legal means; to completely misrepresent the lives and actions of Christians through use of the press, television and films so that their influence and/or freedom is utterly destroyed.

Satan has already cleverly managed to get almost com-plete control of the airwaves, of the news media, of politics, of religion and of education. He has put toge-ther a team of the world's elite: royalty, prime ministers, diplomats and statesmen, international bankers and financiers, university presidents and professors, corporate executives of many of the world's largest companies, actors, actresses, philosophers, publishers, best-selling authors and even "Christian" theologians.

Uniting the world for his takeover are: the New World Order, Globalism, the United Nations and the New Age world religion which teaches reincarnation (a genetic impossibility), astrology, channeling (communication with the dead and with spirits) and Satan's original lie to man - that he can be like God or become a god.

NATIONALISM must be destroyed and replaced with "WORLD" consciousness and the individual reduced to a number. With all banks tied into a global computer system, laser scanning, universal computer bar code, tiny computer chips - everything and everyone will be traceable! The battle for humankind's future is also being waged in the classroom from kindergarten to universities with New Age and one-world teachers shaping young, captive minds, teaching globalism instead of patriotism, situation ethics for moral virtues and disregard of parental authority and validity of religious standards. Young, impressionable minds are being taught New Age meditation, visualization, spirit guides, sex education, alternate life styles, evolution, etc. It is all deliberate, dangerous and destructive!

Being saturated (even the young) with God's word is the only safeguard against being captivated and captured by Satan's lies. It is like going through an enemy minefield; only the Holy Spirit can give discernment as to the true and the false. Sift very carefully everything you see, hear and read and only move with caution and prayer. "Fear not, for I am with you, saith you God."

EVOLUTION

Some say there is no conflict between THE BIBLE and the THEORY of EVOLUTION but actually they are DIAMETRICALLY OPPOSED to each other.

EVOLUTION says everything came into being BY CHANCE: that all living things are related, having a common ancestor- a speck of protoplasm- that suddenly appeared in a primordial slime. This one cell, without a mind or memory, repeatedly divided itself and over millions of years evolved into plants, animals and humans. Each developed unique parts and functions on their own without a designer or creator nor a reason for doing so. No explanation is given as to how they all survived through millions of years while some of their essential parts for living were still evolving.

THE BIBLE says, that an all-wise, all-powerful, all loving GOD CREATED the WORLD and "all that therein is." After years of extensive research, an outstanding scientist has just made the observation that there is only 1/100-billion- trillionth chance that this planet came into being at the right time, in the right position in relation to the sun, moon, stars and the other planets. Everything had to be "fine-tuned" as even a slight variation in size or position would not have allowed the existence of life.

From whence came gases that locked themselves together to form colorless and odorless AIR- a requisite for all life, and why did two of them unite in the correct proportion to form a liquid-WATER-another essential fir life?

THE BIBLE says God created man in His "own "image" (physical eyes, ears, hands, etc.), after His "likeness" (knowing love, hate, jealousy, compassion, etc.) and with all the faculties He possesses today. It was because man broke God's moral laws that sin, sickness, hatred, and wars entered the world.

ALL LIFE will produce LIKE LIFE. Not one case of spontaneous or accidental generation has EVER been observed.

In every species the number of chromosomes in every cell is exactly the same: a house fly has 12, an ox has 38 and man has 46- The only exception is those species which reproduce by sexual attraction-in these the chromosome count is halved in the reproductive cell, e.g. in a man, the sperm has 23 chromosomes and in a woman, the ova has 23 chromosomes so when the two come together there are 46. There is NO EXCEPTION. This is God's law.

EVOLUTIONISTS say the species have evolved over a period of 60,000,000 years. In spite of war, famine and plagues, it m estimated the world population has doubled every 168 years. If this is so and if the human race were 100,000 years old, there would be 4,500,000,000 000,000,000 persons in the world. However, based on today's population, and using the 168-year doubling, we find that 4,500 years ago there would be only handful of people in the world. The FLOOD occurred about 4,500 years ago with only 8 people saved!

Because it is so widely taught and presented by so called learned people (although it is based only on speculation and assumption) many have accepted the theory of evolution WITHOUT doing any real THINKING for THEMSELVES. NONE of the Sciences can prove the theory; no biology, no embryology, not paleontology, anthropology, thermodynamics, or mathematics. PROUD MAN would rather be a REFINED MONKEY than acknowledge being a sinner, accountable for his words, thoughts, and deeds to a HOLY God, and needing a Savior. Instead, they call Him a liar!

- **Rom. 1:20**- *For the invisible things of him from the creation of the world are clearly seen, being understood by the things that are made, even his eternal power and Godhead; so that they are without excuse:*

FAITH

No one can say they do not have faith for the Bible says: "God hath dealt to everyman the measure of faith."(Rom.12:3) We exhibit faith in humans, machinery, and the services they render us but constantly doubt God, even though His word says:

- **Heb. 11:6-** *But without faith it is impossible to please him: for he that cometh to God must believe that he is, and that he is a rewarder of them that diligently seek him.*
- **Heb. 11:1**- Now faith is the substance of things hoped for, the evidence of things not seen.
- **Rom. 10:17**- *So then faith cometh by hearing, and hearing by the word of God.*
- **Eph. 2:8**- *For by grace are ye saved through faith; and that not of yourselves: it is the gift of God:*

FAITH MUST BE EXERCISED, TRIED, and KEPT.

- **2 Thess. 1:3**- *We are bound to thank God always for you, brethren, as it is meet, because that your faith groweth exceedingly, and the*

59

charity of every one of you all toward each other aboundeth;

- **Heb. 10:35-** *Cast not away therefore your confidence, which hath great recompence of reward.*

- **James 1:3-** *Knowing this, that the trying of your faith worketh patience.*

- **1 Pet. 1:7-** *That the trial of your faith, being much more precious than of gold that perisheth, though it be tried with fire, might be found unto praise and honour and glory at the appearing of Jesus Christ:*

- **Mark 11:24-** *Therefore I say unto you, What things soever ye desire, when ye pray, believe that ye receive them, and ye shall have them.*

- **James 1:6-** *But let him ask in faith, nothing wavering. For he that wavereth is like a wave of the sea driven with the wind and tossed.*

- **Matt. 9:29-** *Then touched he their eyes, saying, According to your faith be it unto you.*

- **Matt. 9:22-** *But Jesus turned him about, and when he saw her, he said, Daughter, be of good comfort; thy faith hath made thee whole. And the woman was made whole from that hour.*

- **1 Tim. 6:12-** *Fight the good fight of faith, lay hold on eternal life, whereunto thou art also called, and hast professed a good profession before many witnesses.*

- **2 Tim. 4:7-** *I have fought a good fight, I have finished my course, I have kept the faith:*

(Read the "Faith Chapter" – Hebrews 11)

- **Rom. 1:17**- *The just shall live by faith.*

This is a declaration of great magnitude for it means every facet of life- physical, material, spiritual -must be brought under the dominion of faith: thus God allows testings in each of these realms until His child has conquered all fears and dependence upon people, things and means, and can put complete confidence (faith) in Him and His ability to do and supply ALL THINGS. The 5 senses are the "intercom system within the body but faith is the "wireless" connection with the source of ALL POWER and ALL KNOWLEDGE!

- **Rom. 10:8**- *With the heart God's promises must be believed but the mouth makes the confession. "He shall have whatsoever he saith." (Mark 11:23) Speaking faith in and using the name of JESUS ("All power is given unto me in heaven and in earth.") produces mighty miracles: "In the names of Jesus rise up and walk," "In my name shall they cast our devils," "If ye ask anything in my name, I will do it." Power to conquer sickness, circumstances and demons is IN THE NAME OF JESUS the SON OF GOD.*

FAITH that is REWARDED is comprised of FOUR ESSENTIALS:

1. Asking
2. Believing in heart
3. Confessing with mouth

4. Acting upon confession

- **James 2:26**- *For as the body without the spirit is dead, so faith without works is dead also.*
- **1 John 3:22**- *And whatsoever we ask, we receive of him, because we keep his commandments, and do those things that are pleasing in his sight.*

REWARDS OF FAITH:

- Power to become Sons of God- John 1:12
- Power to do mighty works- John 14:12
- Be kept in perfect peace- Isa. 26:3
- Be kept safe- Prov. 29:25
- Assurance of prayers answered- 1 John 5:14
- Will not be confused- 1 Pet. 2:6

- **Eph. 6:13-16**- *Wherefore take unto you the whole armour of God, that ye may be able to withstand in the evil day, and having done all, to stand. [14] Stand therefore, having your loins girt about with truth, and having on the breastplate of righteousness; [15] And your feet shod with the preparation of the gospel of peace; [16] Above all, taking the shield of faith, wherewith ye shall be able to quench all the fiery darts of the wicked.*

Thus Saith God's Word

FALSE RELIGIONS

- **Matt. 7:15**- *Beware of false prophets, which come to you in sheep's clothing, but inwardly they are ravening wolves.*

Even the average Christian is extremely naive concerning the devil and his tactics, not realizing he is the Master Deceiver who NEVER SLACKENS in his attack on everyone but especially on the Christian and the true Church. EVERY BELIEVER should be on CONSTANT GUARD to judge EVERYTHING he reads and hears as to its conformity to the Bible, not denominational teachings, nor traditions, nor sayings and beliefs of any individual, no matter how prominent he or she is. No human is infallible.

The greater threat a person is to the devil, the greater his concentration to try to destroy from without or from within and to divert. Check the Bible immediately anything that sounds new or different as to it being an isolated verse or one taken out of context for, if it is an important. Belief, God will have spoken concerning it by more than one of His messengers.

- **2 Cor. 13:1**- *This is the third time I am coming to you. In the mouth of two or three witnesses shall every word be established.*
- **Matt. 7:13-14**- *Enter ye in at the strait gate: for wide is the gate, and broad is the way, that leadeth to destruction, and many there be which go in thereat: 14 Because strait is the gate, and narrow is the way, which leadeth unto life, and few there be that find it.*

Not many are willing to "deny themselves, and take up their cross daily and follow" the Lord but they do want to feel PIOUS. Therefore, the devil has been busily serving up "RELIGIOUS STEWS" for thousands of years - putting in sensuality to appeal to the flesh; mysticism for the spirit; intellectualism for the mind; idols, beads, signs, etc. to appeal to the eye and ALL HIGHLY seasoned with LIES. The variety offered on his menu indicates that he strives to please all. Although his specialty is "Eastern" dishes; actually all are concoctions from the same basic recipe: bondage, torment, deadly poison and eternal damnation of the soul.

For centuries the "Eastern" religions have kept millions upon millions in poverty, disease, superstition, and illiteracy. Now they are being "disguised" and offered to the Western world as being beneficial to the body and the mind.

Participation in any form of a pagan philosophy results in some form of oppression or actual possession by the powers of darkness which are operating behind them to ensnare the unwary.

- **Eph. 5:11**- *And have no fellowship with the unfruitful works of darkness, but rather reprove them.*
- **Acts 4:12**- *Neither is there salvation in any other: for there is none other name under heaven given among men, whereby we must be saved.*

REINCARNATION is one of the devil's popular entrees, for it gives people the false hope of having another opportunity to redeem mistakes of past lives, and continue until he attains spiritual perfection. Adherents often claim proof from remembrances of former lives.

Lying spirits, demonic deception, and possession are the answers to these claims. The impersonating demon may have also possessed the earlier in-dividual so could imitate the speech, manner and give even minute details.

- **1 John 4:1-3**- *Beloved, believe not every spirit, but try the spirits whether they are of God: because many false prophets are gone out into the world. ² Hereby know ye the Spirit of God: Every spirit that confesseth that Jesus Christ is come in the flesh is of God: ³ And every spirit that confesseth not that Jesus Christ is come in the flesh is not of God: and this is that spirit of antichrist, whereof ye have heard that it should come; and even now already is it in the world.*

****

Satan delights in using the Bible to lead peo-ple into his traps by using half-truths and taking verses out of context.

One of his half-truths is that the Bible is God's word but that another book or another revelation is equal to it or should be used to explain the scriptures. There is NO NEED for another book, nor further revelation, nor a fuller explanation. How could it be stated more simply?

- **John 20:31**- But these are written, that ye might believe that Jesus is the Christ, the Son of God; and that believing ye might have life through his name.

Those who counterfeit only copy that which is of value and a counterfeit is as close as possible to the true. Usually it is only discernable by experts who have not studied counterfeits but so familiarized themselves with the true that any deviation from it is immediately noted.

- **2 Tim. 2:15**- *Study to shew thyself approved unto God, a workman that needeth not to be ashamed, rightly dividing the word of truth.*
- **Gal. 1:7**- *Which is not another; but there be some that trouble you, and would pervert the gospel of Christ.*

What was the gospel Paul had preached? He outlined it very clearly in Hebrews 6:1-2: that principles of the doctrine of Christ – the main tenets of the faith:

1. Repentance
2. Faith Toward God
3. Baptisms
4. Laying on of Hands
5. Resurrection of Dead
6. Eternal Judgment

1. FOUNDATION OF REPENTANCE FROM DEAD WORKS
   True repentance is to have Godly sorrow for sins and willingness to forsake them.
   - **Luke 13:3**- *I tell you, Nay: but, except ye repent, ye shall all likewise perish.*
   - **Eph. 2:8-9**- *For by grace are ye saved through faith; and that not of yourselves: it is the gift of God: ⁹ Not of works, lest any man should boast.*

2. FAITH TOWARD GOD
   Complete confidence that God will do what He said He would.
   - **1 John 1:9**- *If we confess our sins, he is faithful and just to forgive us our sins, and to cleanse us from all unrighteousness.*

3. THE DOCTRINE OF BAPTISMS
    Notice that this is PLURAL.

    a. Invisible baptism by Holy Spirit at
        conversion.

        - **1 Cor. 12:13**- *For by one
          Spirit are we all baptized into
          one body, whether we be Jews
          or Gentiles, whether we be
          bond or free; and have been
          all made to drink into one
          Spirit.*

    b. Water Baptism

        - **Rom. 6:4**- *Therefore we are
          buried with him by baptism into death: that
          like as Christ was raised up from the dead
          by the glory of the Father, even so we also
          should walk in newness of life.*

    c. Baptism with Holy Ghost

        - **Matt. 3:11**- *I indeed baptize you
          with water unto repentance. but he
          that cometh after me is mightier
          than I, whose shoes I am not worthy
          to bear: he shall baptize you with
          the Holy Ghost, and with fire:*

There are three different Baptizers: The Holy Spirit, a
man, and Jesus.

There are three different Elements: the body of Christ
(the Church); water, and the Holy Ghost.

- (The order of 2 and 3 can be reversed, such as at
  Cornelius' house. Acts 10: 47)

Three different purposes: conversion, outward testimony, and power.

4.   DOCTRINE OF LAYING ON OF HANDS

- **Mark 16:17-18**- *And these signs shall follow them that believe; In my name shall they cast out devils; they shall speak with new tongues; 18 They shall take up serpents; and if they drink any deadly thing, it shall not hurt them; they shall lay hands on the sick, and they shall recover.*

- **Acts 8:5-17**- *Then Philip went down to the city of Samaria, and preached Christ unto them. 6 And the people with one accord gave heed unto those things which Philip spake, hearing and seeing the miracles which he did. 7 For unclean spirits, crying with loud voice, came out of many that were possessed with them: and many taken with palsies, and that were lame, were healed. 8 And there was great joy in that city. 9 But there was a certain man, called Simon, which beforetime in the same city used sorcery, and bewitched the people of Samaria, giving out that himself was some great one: 10 To whom they all gave heed, from the least to the greatest, saying, This man is the great power of God. 11 And to him they had regard, because that of long time he had bewitched them with sorceries. 12 But when they believed Philip preaching the things concerning the kingdom of God, and the name of Jesus Christ, they were baptized, both men and women. 13 Then Simon himself believed also: and when he was baptized, he continued with Philip, and wondered, beholding the miracles and signs which were done. 14 Now when the apostles*

3

*which were at Jerusalem heard that Samaria
had received the word of God, they sent unto
them Peter and John: ¹⁵ Who, when they were
come down, prayed for them, that they might
receive the Holy Ghost: ¹⁶ (For as yet he was
fallen upon none of them: only they were
baptized in the name of the Lord Jesus.) ¹⁷ Then
laid they their hands on them, and they received
the Holy Ghost.*

- **Acts 19:6**- *And when Paul had laid his hands upon
  them, the Holy Ghost came on them; and they spake
  with tongues, and prophesied.*
- **Acts 13:2-3**- *As they ministered to the Lord, and
  fasted, the Holy Ghost said, Separate me Barnabas
  and Saul for the work whereunto I have called them.
  ³ And when they had fasted and prayed, and laid
  their hands on them, they sent them away.*

Three purposes for the laying on of hands are: healing,
ministering the baptism with the Holy Ghost, and
commissioning.

5. RESURRECTION OF THE DEAD

- **1 Cor. 15:20**- *But now is Christ
  risen from the dead, and become the
  firstfruits of them that slept.*
- **Rom. 10:9**- *That if thou shalt confess
  with thy mouth the Lord Jesus, and
  shalt believe in thine heart that God
  hath raised him from the dead, thou
  shalt be saved.*
- **Rev. 20:12-13**- *And I saw the dead,
  small and great, stand before God;*

4

*and the books were opened: and
another book was opened, which is
the book of life: and the dead were
judged out of those things which
were written in the books, according
to their works. [13] And the sea gave up
the dead which were in it; and death
and hell delivered up the dead which
were in them: and they were judged
every man according to their works.*

6. ETERNAL JUDGMENT

- **Matt. 25:42, 45, 46**- *For I was an
  hungred, and ye gave me no meat: I
  was thirsty, and ye gave me no drink:
  [45] Then shall he answer them, saying,
  Verily I say unto you, Inasmuch as ye
  did it not to one of the least of these,
  ye did it not to me. [46] And these shall
  go away into everlasting punishment:
  but the righteous into life eternal.*

A "principle" is a fundamental truth on which others are
founded or from which they spring. These six principles
are the essence of the Bible; God's plan for man in a
"nutshell."

With Jesus as the foundation "For other foundation can
no man lay that is laid, which is Jesus Christ." And the
six "principles" we have God's number of completion –
SEVEN. To be acceptable to God you must accept them
ALL. They are not offered for the individual's (nor the
denomination's) selection, as at a "buffet" - take what
you want and leave the rest. WHO CAN JUDGE GOD

and say which one is not important or not necessary? There is no mention in the "principles" of such as:

- Keeping the Law
- 7th Day Worship
- Only 144,000 going to heaven
- Christ returning invisibly
- Baptism for dead
- Heavenly marriages

a. **Keeping the Law:**

- **Gal. 2:16**- *Knowing that a man is not justified by the works of the law, but by the faith of Jesus Christ, even we have believed in Jesus Christ, that we might be justified by the faith of Christ, and not by the works of the law: for by the works of the law shall no flesh be justified.*
- **Gal. 2:21**- *I do not frustrate the grace of God: for if righteousness come by the law, then Christ is dead in vain.*

****

b. **7th Day Worship**

The FIRST mention of keeping the Sabbath was when God rained down manna from heaven for the Children of Israel in the wilderness. "*Tomorrow is the rest of the holy Sabbath unto the Lord: ... abide ye every man in his place, let no man go out of his place on the seventh day.*" (Ex. 16:23, 29).

- **Acts 1:12**- *Then returned they unto Jerusalem from the mount called Olivet, which is from Jerusalem a sabbath day's journey.*
- **Matt. 12:1**- *At that time Jesus went on the sabbath day through the corn; and his*

disciples were an hungred, and began to pluck the ears of corn and to eat.

- **Mark 2:27-28**- *And he said unto them, The sabbath was made for man, and not man for the sabbath: ²⁸ Therefore the Son of man is Lord also of the sabbath.*

- **Gal. 3:10**- *For as many as are of the works of the law are under the curse: for it is written, Cursed is every one that continueth not in all things which are written in the book of the law to do them.*

If anyone is going to keep part of the law, he or she MUST KEEP IT ALL. To observe the Sabbath according to the actual commandment of Moses means not going out of one's place the whole 7th day; or at the most, not move about more than 2,000 paces; nor to do as much work as rubbing corn together in the hands! WHAT BONDAGE!

- **Gal. 5:1**- *Stand fast therefore in the liberty wherewith Christ hath made us free, and be not entangled again with the yoke of bondage.*

- **Rom. 14:17-18**- *For the kingdom of God is not meat and drink; but righteousness, and peace, and joy in the Holy Ghost. ¹⁸ For he that in these things serveth Christ is acceptable to God, and approved of men.*

Some teach that observing the first day of the week as the Lord's Day "must be the mark (of the Beast) so soon to be imposed!" The Bible teaches very definitely that it is the number of a man, not a day.

- **Rev. 13:16-18**- *And he causeth all, both small and great, rich and poor, free and bond, to receive a mark in their right hand, or in their* *foreheads:* [17] *And that no man might buy or sell, save he that had the mark, or the name of the beast, or the number of his name.* [18] *Here is wisdom. Let him that hath understanding count the number of the beast: for it is the number of a man; and his number is Six hundred threescore and six.*

****

c. **Only 144,000 going to heaven**
    There are others who teach that only a certain very small number, compared with the billions who have lived on this earth, will go to heaven.

    - **Rev. 7:9-10**- *After this I beheld, and, lo, a great multitude, which no man could number, of all nations, and kindreds, and people, and tongues, stood before the throne, and before the Lamb, clothed with white robes, and palms in their hands;* [10] *And cried with a loud voice, saying, Salvation to our God which sitteth upon the throne, and unto the Lamb.*

    ****

d. **Christ Returning Invisibly**
    Jesus is purported to have already come back to this earth "invisibly" whereas, when He ascended on the Mt. of Olives, the two angels declared unto the disciples, "this same Jesus which was taken up from you into heaven, shall SO COME IN LIKE MANNER as ye have seen him go into heaven." (Acts 1:11).
    - **Rev. 1:7**- *Behold, he cometh with clouds;*

*and every eye shall see him, and they also
which pierced him: and all kindreds of the
earth shall wail because of him. Even so,
Amen.*

- **Zech. 14:4**- *And his feet shall stand in that
day upon the mount of Olives, which is
before Jerusalem on the east, and the
mount of Olives shall cleave in the midst
thereof toward the east and toward the
west, and there shall be a very great valley;
and half of the mountain shall remove
toward the north, and half of it toward the
south.*

****

e. **Baptism for Dead**

Others are busily being baptized for the dead
although the Bible consistently teaches that
salvation is a PERSONAL ACCEPTANCE of
Jesus.

- **John 5:24**- *Verily, verily, I say unto you,
He that heareth my word, and believeth on
him that sent me, hath everlasting life, and
shall not come into condemnation; but is
passed from death unto life.*

- **Rom. 4:12**- *And the father of circumcision
to them who are not of the circumcision
only, but who also walk in the steps of that
faith of our father Abraham, which he had
being yet uncircumcised.*

It is just as IMPOSSIBLE to be SAVED for
SOMEONE ELSE as to be BORN for someone
else.

In the 15th Chapter of 1st Corinthians, Paul is
confirming Christ's resurrection in answer to those

who were saying there is no resurrection of the dead, The Sadducees, a sect of the Jews denied the immortality of the soul, yet practiced baptism for the dead. Thus Paul was not confirming their belief but UPBRAIDING them for their incon-sistency.

- **1 Cor. 15:29**- *Else what shall they do which are baptized for the dead, if the dead rise not at all? why are they then baptized for the dead?*

****

f. Heavenly Marriages
Many are being "married for time and eternity" and having plurality of "spiritual wives," thus increasing their kingdom in heaven.

- **Mark 12:24-25**- *And Jesus answering said unto them, Do ye not therefore err, because ye know not the scriptures, neither the power of God? [25] For when they shall rise from the dead, they neither marry, nor are given in marriage; but are as the angels which are in heaven.*

****

- **2 Tim. 4:3**- *For the time will come when they will not endure sound doctrine; but after their own lusts shall they heap to themselves teachers, having itching ears;*
- **2 Thess. 2:1, 3**- *Now we beseech you, brethren, by the coming of our Lord Jesus Christ, and by our gathering together unto him, [3] Let no man deceive you by any means: for that day shall not come, except*

> *there come a falling away first, and that man of sin be revealed, the son of perdition;*

Through the centuries, God's word has been attacked; as have His servants both, even to the burning. Never before the present time, however, has there been such defamation of the Lord Jesus Himself. In the theaters, on television and even from pulpits of so-called Christian churches, the most hideous portrayals of Him and vile accusations and insinuations spoken - bringing Him to the level of the basest of sinners.

- **1 Tim. 4:1-2**- *Now the Spirit speaketh expressly, that in the latter times some shall depart from the faith, giving heed to seducing spirits, and doctrines of devils; ² Speaking lies in hypocrisy; having their conscience seared with a hot iron;*
- **2 Cor. 11:13-15**- *For such are false apostles, deceitful workers, transforming themselves into the apostles of Christ. ¹⁴ And no marvel; for Satan himself is transformed into an angel of light. ¹⁵ Therefore it is no great thing if his ministers also be transformed as the ministers of righteousness; whose end shall be according to their works.*

A centuries-old religion is now gaining many followers in Europe and America spreading hate and division, also the lie that Christianity is only for a certain race (color) of people. EVERYONE in the world is a descendant of ADAM and GOD makes NO DISTINCTION between them. He "*so love the WORLD that He gave HIS ONLY BEGOTTEN SON, that WHOSOEVER believeth on HIM should not perish but have EVERLASTING LIFE.*" (**John**

3:16). "God is love" and He causes He true believers to show that love and compassion. The devil incites hatred, jealousy, and killing. (See Jews).

<u>FAMILY</u>

Few people realize that being a parent entails an AWESOME responsibility and accountability for the new life (bone of my bone and flesh of my flesh" will live forever, either in heaven or hell.

To provide every physical necessity, along with a varying amount of luxuries; to give the best of education; and though he or she may rise to world-wide fame or amass a fortune, the parent has utterly failed if the reason for life and the accountability to God has not been taught.

- **Ecc. 12:13-14**- *Let us hear the conclusion of the whole matter: Fear God, and keep his commandments: for this is the whole duty of man. [14] For God shall bring every work into judgment, with every secret thing, whether it be good, or whether it be evil.*
- **Mark 8:36**- *For what shall it profit a man, if he shall gain the whole world, and lose his own soul?*

The learning process starts early by copying the actions as well and as repeating the words of those around, as well as taking on their thinking patterns. Is it any wonder there is a juvenile delinquency problem when so many parents have been careless of their words and actions and have delegated the raising of their children to babysitters, schools and television?

No child will ever respect a parent who either

In word or deed says: "Do as I say, not as I do." Smoking, drinking, swearing parents who argue and are disrespectful to each other, gender argumentative and disrespectful children who will also smoke, drink and swear. It is impossible to go against God's law:

- **Gal. 6:7**- *Be not deceived; God is not mocked: for whatsoever a man soweth, that shall he also reap.*

To be successful, parents should sow good seed by so ordering their own lives to be patterns for their children to follow.

- **Prov. 22:6**- *Train up a child in the way he should go: and when he is old, he will not depart from it.*

Satan caused violence and death in the first home and now in these end days he is again wag-ing a full-scale attack on not only the par-ents but on the children. Violence on the TV causes violence in the street and even little children are committing terrible crimes. Tobacco and liquor are so glamorized and attract-ively advertised that hundreds of thousands of boys and girls are becoming addicts.

Only the husband and wife who have had a genu-ine experience of salvation and filling of the Holy Spirit will be able to stand the on-slaught -sexually, emotionally, financially, morally and spiritually, (See "Holy Spirit") They should be united and put the training of their children "in the fear (reverential love) of the Lord," as their prime objective, for years pass so swiftly and they are soon gone from the home. (See "Marriage")

Powerful forces are working to get children out of the home at the earliest age possible so that their thinking and actions can be controlled. God's word, His name and influence have been replaced in the classrooms of all levels with evolutionary and atheistic teaching.

Parents should teach their children as early as possible that they are players in the game of life; having them sign up on God's side by asking Jesus to be their Savior-their Captain. As they grow in understanding, keep adding to the list of His rules and requirements; being sure THEY THEMSELVES OBEY the RULES, too,

Teach the Ten Commandments and that those who break them are soon broken BY them. (Deu.5:7-21)

- **Prov. 1:7**- *The fear of the LORD is the beginning of knowledge: but fools despise wisdom and instruction.*
- **Prov. 15:3**- *The eyes of the LORD are in every place, beholding the evil and the good.*

They should know as early as possible that God sees everything they do and hears every-thing they say and think.

- **Prov. 16:32**- *He that is slow to anger is better than the mighty; and he that ruleth his spirit than he that taketh a city.*
- **Prov. 22:1**- *A good name is rather to be chosen than great riches, and loving favour rather than silver and gold.*
- **Prov. 15:5**- *A fool despiseth his father's instruction: but he that regardeth reproof is prudent.*
- **Prov. 1:10**- *My son, if sinners entice thee, consent thou not.*
- **Prov. 3:9**- *Honour the LORD with thy substance, and with the firstfruits of all thine increase:*
- **Prov. 3:6**- *In all thy ways acknowledge him, and he shall direct thy paths.*
- **Rom. 12:21**- *Be not overcome of evil, but overcome evil with good.*

- **1 Thess. 5:22**- *Abstain from all appearance of evil.*

- **Prov. 20:1**- *Wine is a mocker, strong drink is raging: and whosoever is deceived thereby is not wise.*

- **Prov. 6:16-19**- These six things doth the LORD hate: yea, seven are an abomination unto him:
    1. A proud look,
    2. A lying tongue
    3. Hands that shed innocent blood
    4. A heart that deviseth wicked imaginations
    5. Feet that be swift in running to mischief
    6. A false witness that speaketh lies
    7. He that soweth discord among brethren.

Children must be disciplined - not in wrath but in love for:

- **Prov. 22:15**- *Foolishness is bound in the heart of a child; but the rod of correction shall drive it far from him.*

- **Prov. 17:21**- *He that begetteth a fool doeth it to his sorrow: and the father of a fool hath no joy.*

- **Prov. 13:24**- *He that spareth his rod hateth his son: but he that loveth him chasteneth him betimes.*

- **Prov. 29:17**- *Correct thy son, and he shall give thee rest; yea, he shall give delight unto thy soul.*

- **Col. 3:20**- *Children, obey your parents in all things: for this is well pleasing unto the Lord.*

- **Eph. 6:11**- *Fathers, provoke not your children*

to anger. Lest they be discouraged.

- **Prov. 20:11**- *Even a child is known by his doings, whether his work be pure, and whether it be right.*

Young people should know, who will not be saved," "These will have their part in the lake of fire:

- The fearful- fearing to stake a stand for Jesus because of what people will say, think, or do.
- The unbelieving-in Jesus and God's word.
- Murderers-includes those who murder themselves (suicide)
- Sorcerers- includes using tarot cards and Ouija boards, etc.
- Witchcraft- All liars -thieves
- The effeminate- homosexuals
- Drunkards- use of all forms of liquor
- Those who are filled with hatred, wrath, strife, envyings, and such like.

In every game there are at least two sides and the whole policy of the opposition is to outwit; block as many plays as possible, and, of course, ultimately defeat. No matter what the game, the player has always to be alert, watching the opposition's move and planning his own defense and hopefully make a gain.

The leader of the opposing team in the game of life is none other than the devil himself. He, his demons, and those humans who have been won to his side, never play fairly but lie, cheat and deceive - calling evil good and good evil, and making sin look attractive and desirable instead of ugly, degenerate and with power to bind and destroy.

Loyalty to one's team should be understood. Sad to say, there are many who signed up on the Lord's team who are constantly on the devil's territory, making goals for his cause. No cap-tain would keep such a player on the team. Jesus DEMANDS complete loyalty, too,

No one could ever stand against Satan if Captain Jesus had not already won the victory over him; and only as His coaching instructions are followed (And they overcame him by the blood of the Lamb, and by the word of their testimony) can His protection, blessing and victory be had.

This is NO MAKE-BELIEVE GAME, nor "just for fun."

- **1 Pet. 5:8**- *Be sober, be vigilant; because your adversary the devil, as a roaring lion, walketh about, seeking whom he may devour:*

Players do their best when people are watching and urging them on to victory. Our grandstand is filled with celebrities and heroes, whose names and deeds have been revered through hundreds and thousands of years, who are all cheering us on to victory: Noah, Abraham, Joseph, Moses, David, Peter, Paul, James,

John, et.al. These all were in the arena in combat with the devil, and against great odds, but by faith and trust in God, they won and are with Him now and forever more.

- **Phil. 3:14**- *I press toward the mark for the prize of the high calling of God in Christ Jesus.*

What a time it will be when the millions of the redeemed throughout all ages gather for God's Award Presentation Ceremony with the rewards and crowns presented to those who were faithful and overcame the devil; those did great exploits for the King of Kings!

- **Rev. 2:10**- *Fear none of those things which thou shalt suffer: behold, the devil shall cast some of you into prison, that ye may be tried; and ye shall have tribulation ten days: be thou faithful unto death, and I will give thee a crown of life.*

Parents, take time to be with your children; teach them good manners; to be polite to all and especially to be loving, kind and helpful to every member of the family and to do everything well for God's glory. Encourage constantly and instill responsibility and trust rather than criticizing and showing distrust. Let them know that rock music and most television programs are weapons of the enemy to undermine Christian moral values, to ensnare and destroy. Read the Bible and pray with them daily. If you are excited about God and going to heaven, they will catch your enthusiasm.

RECIPE FOR A HAPPY HOME

- 4 cups of love
- 2 cups of loyalty
- 3 cups of forgiveness
- 1 cup of friendship
- 5 spoons of hope

-
- 2 spoons of tenderness
- 4 quarts of faith
- 1 barrel of laughter

Take love and loyalty, mix in thoroughly with faith. Blend it with tenderness, kindness and understanding. Add friendship and hope; sprin-kle abundantly with laughter. Garnish with hugs and kisses. Serve generous portions daily.

- **1 John 3:1**- *Behold, what manner of love the Father hath bestowed upon us, that we should be called the sons of God: therefore the world knoweth us not, because it knew him not.*

The Christian family should be the example of the Family of God. The father has the great responsi-bility of demonstrating love, encouragement and discipline in the family. He should realize the magnitude of his role; not demanding respect by shouting commands to his children and exacting submission from his wife, but by so ordering his O\l/n life, showing sincere love and interest, that he 11Jins the respect, confidence and love of his family.

(Prayer of father) God, forgive all my sins. I am truly sorry I have not represented Thee well to my family. Help me from this minute on to live a holy life, being a better example that they might respect, love and obey Thee as a Fa-ther although they do not see Thee. Help me to be honest and sincere with my discipline that they might know that as a Father, You have to punish sin or You would not be just. Help me to teach them Thy word that they might accept Je-sus as Savior as soon as possible. Lord, m a y our family be united in heaven without the loss of one. Holy Spirit, please guide me. AMEN.

(Prayer of mother) Jesus, forgive all my past. I give Thee my life. Help me to do even the smallest or most monotonous task as unto Thee, knowing that Thou wilt not let it go unrewarded. Make me the mother I should be to show forth Thy love to my family. Help me to guide them to guard their heart above all things, considering it a garden where all the graces grow - kindness, patience and the love of that which is good; and that as soon as a bad thought enters or a bad habit starts, it should be pulled out by the root immediately, knowing that like a weed, it will soon destroy the good. Let them remember me not as a slave to fashion and the pleasures of this world, but rather as Thy faithful follower who has crucified the desires for this world and whose prayers will follow them all their days until death separates us. AMEN.

(Prayer of son or daughter) Jesus, I give You my

life. I accept You as my Savior. Help me to always bring honor to our team and to You as my Captain, knowing that to neglect my studies and my work and to cheat is actually being dishonest to myself and I will be the loser. Help me to overcome evil that when I stand before Your throne You can reward me with a beautiful crown. Thank You for loving me. I love You. AMEN.

FEAR

There are good fears and bad. The latter kind comes
from wrong believing and open the door to doubt and
hinder the flow of God's power. They are from the devil
and should be resisted as they cause mental and physical
TORMENT.

The Greek word "*delia*" is for a cowardly fear; not being
able to face a problem, but instead, running from it. This
results from lack of discipline and maturity.

Then there is the "*phobos*" fear of people or things,
based on lies. The best way to be free from Satanic
attack is to live in the truth - to be open - to be "for real."

There is a fear that all should have - the FEAR OF THE
LORD. This is NOT to be in terror of GOD but to be in
AWE of and FILLED WITH REVERENCE FOR Him.

This fear that changes and motivates the entire life,

results from coming into the presence of the Lord; seeing, by faith, His glorious majesty; strength and power; His holiness; His infinite love and mercy; and realizing that He is the source and supplier of everything we need now and forever.

- **Deut. 4:10**- *Specially the day that thou stoodest before the LORD thy God in Horeb, when the LORD said unto me, Gather me the people together, and I will make them hear my words, that they may learn to fear me all the days that they shall live upon the earth, and that they may teach their children.*

There are great rewards for this fear:

- It is the beginning of wisdom."
- "It is the beginning of knowledge."
- It is a fountain of life."
- "It prolongeth days."
- "In it is strong confidence."
- "By it are riches and honor."
    - **Psa. 34:9**- *O fear the LORD, ye his saints: for there is no want to them that fear him.*
    - **Psa. 145:19**- *He will fulfil the desire of them that fear him: he also will hear their cry, and will save them.*
    - **Psa. 34:7**- *The angel of the LORD encampeth round about them that fear him, and delivereth them.*
    - **1 John 4:18**- *There is no fear in love; but perfect love casteth out fear: because fear*

hath torment. He that feareth is not made perfect in love.

- **Psa. 34:4**- *I sought the LORD, and he heard me, and delivered me from all my fears.*
- **2 Tim. 1:7**- *For God hath not given us the spirit of fear; but of power, and of love, and of a sound mind.*
- **Isa. 41:10**- *Fear thou not; for I am with thee: be not dismayed; for I am thy God: I will strengthen thee; yea, I will help thee; yea, I will uphold thee with the right hand of my righteousness.*
- **Psa. 27:1**- *The LORD is my light and my salvation; whom shall I fear? the LORD is the strength of my life; of whom shall I be afraid?*
- **Psa. 23:4**- *Yea, though I walk through the valley of the shadow of death, I will fear no evil: for thou art with me; thy rod and thy staff they comfort me.*
- **Psa. 56:11**- *In God have I put my trust: I will not be afraid what man can do unto me.*
- **Prov. 8:13**- *The fear of the LORD is to hate evil: pride, and arrogancy, and the evil way, and the froward mouth, do I hate.*

There is a fear GOD will NOT TOLERATE - fear of taking a stand for Him before the world, and He places it at the top of the list of causes for being lost.

- **Rev. 21: 8**- *But the fearful, and unbelieving, and the abominable, and murderers, and* whoremongers, and sorcerers, and idolaters, and all liars, shall have their part in the lake which burneth with fire and brimstone: which is the second death.

- **<u>Matt. 10:33</u>**- *But whosoever shall deny me before men, him will I also deny before my Father which is in heaven.*

- **<u>Mal. 3:16-17</u>**- *Then they that feared the LORD spake often one to another: and the LORD hearkened, and heard it, and a book of remembrance was written before him for them that feared the LORD, and that thought upon his name. [17] And they shall be mine, saith the LORD of hosts, in that day when I make up my jewels; and I will spare them, as a man spareth his own son that serveth him.*

- **<u>Prov. 23:17</u>**- *Let not thine heart envy sinners: but be thou in the fear of the LORD all the day long.*

FINANCES

The first of God's Ten Commandments is: *"Thou shalt have no other gods before me."* (**Ex. 20:3**). But, without question, MONEY is the GOD of THIS WORLD! People everywhere are so concerned about accumulating it and the material goods it buys that it behooves Christians to be watchful that they do not bow their knees also.

- **1 Tim. 6:10**- *For the love of money is the root of all evil: which while some coveted after, they have erred from the faith, and pierced themselves through with many sorrows.*
- **Ecc. 5:10**- *He that loveth silver shall not be satisfied with silver; nor he that loveth abundance with increase: this is also vanity.*
- **James 5:3**- *Your gold and silver is cankered;*

76

and the rust of them shall be a witness against you, and shall eat your flesh as it were fire. Ye have heaped treasure together for the last days.

- **Luke 12:20**- *But God said unto him, Thou fool, this night thy soul shall be required of thee: then whose shall those things be, which thou hast provided?*

The Lord knows His children's needs and He wants to supply them. To have them in poverty brings no glory to Him for His word says:

- **3 John 1:2**- *Beloved, I wish above all things that thou mayest prosper and be in health, even as thy soul prospereth.*
- **Prov. 8:21**- *That I may cause those that love me to inherit substance; and I will fill their treasures.*

Therefore, your part is to love Him and see that your soul prospers; then God will do His part.

- **Matt. 6:33**- *But seek ye first the kingdom of God, and his righteousness; and all these things shall be added unto you.*
- **Psa. 84:11**- *For the LORD God is a sun and shield: the LORD will give grace and glory: no good thing will he withhold from them that walk uprightly.*
- **Psa. 34:9**- *O fear the LORD, ye his saints: for there is no want to them that fear him.*
- **Psa. 37:25**- *I have been young, and now am*

old; yet have I not seen the righteous
forsaken, nor his seed begging bread.

- **Psa. 1:1-3**- *Blessed is the man that walketh
not in the counsel of the ungodly, nor
standeth in the way of sinners, nor sitteth in
the seat of the scornful. ² But his delight is in
the law of the LORD; and in his law doth he
meditate day and night. ³ And he shall be like
a tree planted by the rivers of water, that
bringeth forth his fruit in his season; his leaf
also shall not wither; and whatsoever he
doeth shall prosper.*

- **Rom. 12:11**- *Not slothful in business; fervent
in spirit; serving the Lord;*

- **Col. 3:23-24**- *And whatsoever ye do, do it
heartily, as to the Lord, and not unto men;
²⁴ Knowing that of the Lord ye shall receive
the reward of the inheritance: for ye serve
the Lord Christ.*

You must be obedient in giving God your tithe. Be as
careful with His money as you are with your own; invest
it where it will bring the greatest return for Him.

- **Mal. 3:10-11**- *Bring ye all the tithes into the
storehouse, that there may be meat in mine
house, and prove me now herewith, saith
the LORD of hosts, if I will not open you the
windows of heaven, and pour you out a
blessing, that there shall not be room enough
to receive it. ¹¹ And I will rebuke the devourer
for your sakes, and he shall not destroy the
fruits of your ground; neither shall your vine*

cast her fruit before the time in the field, saith the LORD of hosts.

- **Prov. 3:9**- *Honour the LORD with thy substance, and with the firstfruits of all thine increase:*

- **Luke 6:38**- *Give, and it shall be given unto you; good measure, pressed down, and shaken together, and running over, shall men give into your bosom. For with the same measure that ye mete withal it shall be measured to you again.*

This is a divine law: the more you give, the more you receive. This applies not only to money but giving of your time and talents for causes that BRING HIM HONOR. Give of yourself in prayer and you will be given answers to prayer; Give of yourself to God by fasting and He will in turn bless you with physical strength and health. Give faithfully to God1s work and He will fill your life with blessings.

- **2 Cor. 9:6**- *But this I say, He which soweth sparingly shall reap also sparingly; and he which soweth bountifully shall reap also bountifully.*

(Prayer) Lord Jesus, I put my trust in Thee for my soul's salvation and the providing of my ne-cessities. Give me wisdom in all that I do that I might bring glory to Thy name. I trust and thank Thee for the solution of my problem. I will give Thee the tithe and offerings that are due Thee along with my time and talents. AMEN.

- **Mark 11:24**- *Therefore I say unto you,*

Thus Saith God's Word

*What things soever ye desire, when ye pray,
believe that ye receive them, and ye shall
have them.* (See **"Faith"**).

FORGIVENESS- GUILT

GUILT, like a vicious animal, stalks its prey; driving its victims to drink, drugs, illicit sex, psychiatric wards, murder and suicide; and will TORMENT the soul for eternity.

Daily, sin is being more glamorized but its re-sults are also increasing; 1 out of 3 hospital beds has a mental patient. Man will go to any means, even spending fortunes, to cover or get rid of guilt but RELEASE ONLY COMES from GOD for His are the laws that have been broken.

- **Num. 32:23**- *But if ye will not do so, behold, ye have sinned against the LORD: and be sure your sin will find you out.*

King David acknowledged his sin was ever be-fore him. Day and night he felt God's hand heavy upon him. When he kept silent and did not confess it, even his "bones waxed old."

When he humbled himself, acknowledged his
transgressions, sought and received the Lord's
forgiveness he could say:

- **Psa. 40:1-3**- *I waited patiently for the LORD;
  and he inclined unto me, and heard my cry.
  ² He brought me up also out of an horrible
  pit, out of the miry clay, and set my feet
  upon a rock, and established my goings.
  ³ And he hath put a new song in my mouth,
  even praise unto our God: many shall see it,
  and fear, and shall trust in the LORD.*
- **Isa. 1:18**- *Come now, and let us reason
  together, saith the LORD: though your sins
  be as scarlet, they shall be as white as snow;
  though they be red like crimson, they shall
  be as wool.*
- **Col. 1:14**- *In whom we have redemption
  through his blood, even the forgiveness of
  sins:*
- **Psa. 86:5**- *For thou, Lord, art good, and
  ready to forgive; and plenteous in mercy
  unto all them that call upon thee.*
- **Prov. 28:13**- *He that covereth his sins shall
  not prosper: but whoso confesseth and
  forsaketh them shall have mercy.*
- **1 John 1:9**- *If we confess our sins, he is
  faithful and just to forgive us our sins, and
  to cleanse us from all unrighteousness.*
- **Isa. 43:25**- *I, even I, am he that blotteth out
  thy transgressions for mine own sake, and
  will not remember thy sins.*
- **Psa. 103:12**- *As far as the east is from the
  west, so far hath he removed our
  transgressions from us.*

Thus Saith God's Word

FORGIVENESS of MAN to FELLOWMAN

- **Matt. 6:14-15**- *For if ye forgive men their trespasses, your heavenly Father will also forgive you: [15] But if ye forgive not men their trespasses, neither will your Father forgive your trespasses.*
- **Eph. 4:32**- *And be ye kind one to another, tenderhearted, forgiving one another, even as God for Christ's sake hath forgiven you.*

If you have unconfessed sin in your heart and it has been haunting you, why not get rid of it right now? Why let the devil torment you any longer? God offers forgiveness; why not gladly receive it?

If you have been carrying a grudge against someone, or even planning now to get even, why not confess it right now and let God do the "getting even" for you? *"Vengeance is mine; I will repay, saith the Lord."* (**Rom. 12:19**).

DEAR JESUS, have mercy on me, a sinner. I am truly sorry for my sins. Forgive my past- every thought, word and deed. I accept You as my lord and Savior. Make me Your child. Take away all sinful desires and create in me a new heart, I forgive everyone who has wronged me and I thank You for forgiving me and cleansing me by Your blood shed on the cross for me. I believe You have heard this prayer and I thank Vou for letting me start all over. I accept Your pardon and Your peace. Amen.

- **Luke 15:10**- *Likewise, I say unto you, there*

83

is joy in the presence of the angels of God over one sinner that repenteth.

As God has now forgiven your sins, cast them in to the depths of the sea, (At one place in the South Pacific, the ocean floor is as deep as Mt. Everest is high!) and has already forgotten them; then you cast them away from your memory and claim His promise -

- **Psa. 32:1**- *Blessed is he whose transgression is forgiven, whose sin is covered.*
- **Rom. 8:1**- *There is therefore now no condemnation to them which are in Christ Jesus, who walk not after the flesh, but after the Spirit.* (See "**Holy Spirit**")

<u>GUIDANCE</u>

Everyone desires to know the future. The devil's books on guidance - how to know one's future, horoscopes, ESP, interpretation of dreams, etc. are everywhere. Young and old are caught up in fortune-telling, séances and ouija boards. High officials consult "prophets" and "prophetesses" and parents follow guidance of ungodly counsellors to rear their children and reap heartbreak.

Even Christians are searching madly for guidance. John Wesley warned: "Do not hastily ascribe all things to God. Do not easily suppose dreams, voices, impressions, visions or revelations to be from God. They may be from Him, they may be from nature, they may be from the devil. Therefore, believe not every spirit but try the spirits, whether they be from God."

Beware of accepting prophecy from someone else for guidance of your life. God always deals with the individual, He may confirm through prophecy what He has already spoken to the person.

- **<u>Psa. 32:8</u>**- *I will instruct thee and teach thee in the way which thou shalt go: I will guide thee with mine eye.*

God is the only one who knows your past, present and future; your capabilities and needs. He alone can open and close all doors so your prayer should be:

- **<u>Psa. 27:11</u>**- *Teach me thy way, O LORD, and lead me in a plain path, because of mine enemies.*

God will not force His will on anyone; so be teachable; sincere; yielded and watchful. His leading will be in accord with His Word; be reasonable and bear witness with your spirit.

- **<u>Rom. 12:2</u>**- *And be not conformed to this world: but be ye transformed by the renewing of your mind, that ye may prove what is that good, and acceptable, and perfect, will of God.*
- **<u>Psa. 25:9</u>**- *The meek will he guide in judgment: and the meek will he teach his way.*
- **<u>Prov. 3:5-6-</u>** *Trust in the LORD with all thine heart; and lean not unto thine own understanding. ⁶ In all thy ways acknowledge him, and he shall direct thy paths.*

- **Psa. 25:4-5**- *Shew me thy ways, O LORD; teach me thy paths. [5] Lead me in thy truth, and teach me: for thou art the God of my salvation; on thee do I wait all the day.*
- **Psa. 37:23**- *The steps of a good man are ordered by the LORD: and he delighteth in his way.*
- **Psa. 23:3**- *He restoreth my soul: he leadeth me in the paths of righteousness for his name's sake.*

[(Read all of Psalm 23)

- **Psa. 48:14**- *For this God is our God for ever and ever: he will be our guide even unto death.*
- **Psa. 37:5**- *Commit thy way unto the LORD; trust also in him; and he shall bring it to pass.*

A good general rule for guidance is:

1. Does it conform to the Word of God? *"Thy word is a lamp unto my feet and a light unto my path."* (**Psa. 119: 105**).
2. Does the Spirit bear witness within you?
3. Have circumstances been made favorable?

Don't be impatient. We do not have a blossom the day after the seed is planted nor can we force open the petals of a rose without ruining the flower.

- **2 Cor. 5:7**- *(For we walk by faith, not by sight:)*
- **Psa. 31:3**- *For thou art my rock and my fortress; therefore for thy name's sake lead me, and guide me.*
- **Psa. 107:28-30**- *Then they cry unto the LORD in their trouble, and he bringeth them out of their distresses. 29 He maketh the storm a calm, so that the waves thereof are still. 30 Then are they glad because they be quiet; so he bringeth them unto their desired haven.*

Jesus knew how needful guidance would be, therefore he COMMANDED His followers to be baptized with the Holy Ghost. *"Howbeit when He, the Spirit of Truth, is come, He will guide you into all truth."* (**John 16:13**).

- **Rom. 8:14**- *For as many as are led by the Spirit of God, they are the sons of God.*

(See "**Holy Spirit**")

HEALING

- **Psa. 139:14**- *I will praise thee; for I am fearfully and wonderfully made: marvellous are thy works; and that my soul knoweth right well.*

If David had even a fraction of the knowledge about the human body as we, he would really have been awed. The cell, simplest form of life, is more complicated than the most complicated man-made thing. The average number of living cells in a human adult is 60 thousand billion.

In EACH of these is something called DNA that has the genetic blueprint for the entire body, yet is also highly specialized to do its own purpose.

Each of the 10 billion BRAIN cells is more complicated than the telephone system in a huge metropolis. The HEART is the size of a man's fist yet daily pumps 2,000 gallons of blood through 60,000 miles of blood vessels; not on-ly distributing food but at the same time gathering waste. The EYE is the most intricate camera ever made; the HAND -the most versatile instrument on earth. On today's market, to construct even a semblance of the body, would cost in access of $6,000,000.00.

If God designed and created such a marvelous house for the soul to dwell with the Holy Spirit during its stay on this earth, it stands to reason He is interested in its functioning properly and being carefully taken care of.

- **1 Cor. 6:19**- *What? know ye not that your body is the temple of the Holy Ghost which is in you, which ye have of God, and ye are not your own?*

We are "workers together with Him" so if we do our part to maintain the body properly, He will fulfill His part.

- **3 John 1:2-** *Beloved, I wish above all things that thou mayest prosper and be in health, even as thy soul prospereth.*
- **Ex. 15:26**- *And said, If thou wilt diligently hearken to the voice of the LORD thy God, and wilt do that which is right in his sight, and wilt give ear to his commandments, and keep all his statutes, I will put none of these diseases upon thee, which I have brought upon the Egyptians: for I am the LORD that healeth thee.*

Therefore, the first step toward healing, or the maintaining of good health, is to search one's self to see if His commandments have been obeyed and if time and effort have been put on the prospering of the soul: Bible reading, prayer, praising, etc., for the Word says to do these, fearing the Lord and departing from evil, *"shall be health to thy navel, and marrow to thy bones."* (**Prov. 3:1-8).**

- **Psa. 34:19-** *Many are the afflictions of the righteous: but the LORD delivereth him out of them all.*
- **Psa. 103:2-3** *Bless the LORD, O my soul, and forget not all his benefits: ³ Who forgiveth all thine iniquities; who healeth all thy diseases;*
- **Acts 10:38-** *How God anointed Jesus of Nazareth with the Holy Ghost and with power: who went about doing good, and healing all that were oppressed of the devil; for God was with him.*
- **Matt. 8:16-17-** *When the even was come, they brought unto him many that were possessed with devils: and he cast out the spirits with his word, and healed all that were sick: ¹⁷ That it might be fulfilled which was spoken by Esaias the prophet, saying, Himself took our infirmities, and bare our sicknesses.*

There are 729 verses in the New Testament that have something to do with healing in them. Jesus healed while on this earth and He is "the same yesterday, today, and forever." There were healings in the Old Testament also. Therefore, would God do for the people who lived during the period of the writing of the Old and New Testaments, what He will not do for those living since?

Christ's death bought BOTH SALVATION and HEALING for ALL but only those who claim salvation and act upon it are saved; the same is true of healing. The multitude thronged around Jesus but the ONE who claimed healing and with believing faith touched Him, received it.

- **Mark 5:28-** *For she said, If I may touch but his clothes, I shall be whole.*

Those who teach it is not God's will to heal now -that sickness brings glory to Him, still go to physicians, take medicine and do everything possible trying to become well. It is God's will to heal!

- **Matt. 8:2**- *And, behold, there came a leper and worshipped him, saying, Lord, if thou wilt, thou canst make me clean.*

FAITH is the key to all of God's blessings. The first thing a sick believer should do is go to The Great Physician; He designed and made the body; He knows how to repair it.

- **James 5:14-16**- *Is any sick among you? let him call for the elders of the church; and let them pray over him, anointing him with oil in the name of the Lord:* [15] *And the prayer of faith shall save the sick, and the Lord shall raise him up; and if he have committed sins, they shall be forgiven him.* [16] *Confess your faults one to another, and pray one for another, that ye may be healed. The effectual fervent prayer of a righteous man availeth much.*

God alone forgives sin but confession of faults to others is humbling.

- **James 4:10**- *Humble yourselves in the sight of the Lord, and he shall lift you up.*

The SICK PERSON calling for prayer shows his faith; the ANNOINTING WITH OIL (not typifying the use of medicine as some teach) is a symbol of the Holy Spirit and an act of obedience on the: part of the ones praying "the prayer of faith" and GOD's part is to raise him up.

Sometimes the raising up is instantaneous but it usually comes gradually as with the planting of a seed.

- **Mark 11:24**- *Therefore I say unto you, What things soever ye desire, when ye pray, believe that ye receive them, and ye shall have them.*
- **Heb. 11:1**- *Now faith is the substance of things hoped for, the evidence of things not seen.*

Therefore, at the time a person is prayed for, the answer is as a tangible substance and God should be thanked and praised for it. The pe-riod between the praying and the actual visual evidence is the "trial of faith" which "is more precious than gold;" believing God's word although none of the five senses testify to it.

- **Psa. 27:1**- *The LORD is my light and my salvation; whom shall I fear? the LORD is the strength of my life; of whom shall I be* *afraid?*

After consulting a doctor, one would not imme-diately go to another; disregarding the first's diagnosis or not allowing time for his method or medicine to have effect. Jesus should re-ceive the SAME RESPECT.

- **James 1:6-7**- *But let him ask in faith, nothing wavering. For he that wavereth is like a wave of the sea driven with the wind and tossed.[7] For let not that man think that he shall receive any thing of the Lord.*
- **1 John 3:22**- *And whatsoever we ask, we receive of him, because we keep his commandments, and do those things that are pleasing in his sight.*

Jesus said: "These signs shall follow them that believer; ...they shall lay hands on the sick, and they SHALL RECOVER." Mark 16:18). There is no limitation to apostles' hands as some teach, or that sign gifts ceased with their death.

- **Matt. 18:19**- *Again I say unto you, That if two of you shall agree on earth as touching any thing that they shall ask, it shall be done for them of my Father which is in heaven.*

Healing comes when there is ND ANXIETY of mind, but ABSOLUTE CONFIDENCE in His ability and love.

As with Christ's " instructions on salvation "Go and sin no more," He told the impotent man:

94

- **John 5:14**- *Afterward Jesus findeth him in the temple, and said unto him, Behold, thou art made whole: sin no more, lest a worse thing come unto thee.*

Not only a person who has been healed, but all should check their lives as to the proper care of the body and spirit.

- **1 Cor. 6:20**- *For ye are bought with a price: therefore glorify God in your body, and in your spirit, which are God's.*
- **1 Cor. 3:17**- *If any man defile the temple of God, him shall God destroy; for the temple of God is holy, which temple ye are.*
- **1 Cor. 9:27**- *But I keep under my body, and bring it into subjection: lest that by any means, when I have preached to others, I myself should be a castaway.*
- **1 Cor. 11:27-30**- *Wherefore whosoever shall eat this bread, and drink this cup of the Lord, unworthily, shall be guilty of the body and blood of the Lord. [28] But let a man examine himself, and so let him eat of that bread, and drink of that cup. [29] For he that eateth and drinketh unworthily, eateth and drinketh damnation to himself, not discerning the Lord's body. [30] For this cause many are weak and sickly among you, and many sleep.*
- **1 Cor. 10:31**- *Whether therefore ye eat, or drink, or whatsoever ye do, do all to the glory of God.*

No alcohol in any form or amount should be consumed for it destroys brain cells, affects the heart, liver, vision, speech, coordination and enslaves. (See <u>Alcohol</u>)

No tobacco should be used. (See <u>Smoking</u>).

- **Phil. 4:5**- *Let your moderation be known unto all men. The Lord is at hand.*

This includes food as 40% of adult Americans are overweight, doubling the possibilities of heart attacks and strokes. Every 20 lbs. of extra weight shortens the life expectance by 7 years.

Coffee, tea, cola, cocoa and chocolate are loaded with a poisonous stimulant drug called caffeine, which drives the adrenal glands into such a frenzy of activity that it robs the liver of its store of glycogen for energy. Excessive caffeine intake is especially harmful to kidneys, which must eliminate the poisonous drug; and to the liver, which becomes overwhelmed in its attempt to detoxify the caffeine. Some symptom of the poisoning are: faintness, headache, restlessness, insomnia, etc. In tests, 13 out of 14 women who drank 7 or more cups of coffee daily had miscarriages, still births or fetal deaths. Women drinkers of 1 cup daily have 25% greater risk of bladder cancer. Children and teenagers who consume cola drinks and chocolate candy are damaging their nervous system as well as the liver and kidneys.

Mental health results from obedience to His commands to think upon things that are true, pure, honest, etc. (Phil.4:8) This calls for strict discipline of what is read and looked at. "Fret not thyself because of evil doers, neither be envious against the workers of iniquity," and "Casting all your care upon Him." (See **Thoughts**).

Fear, worry and jealousy have a detrimental effect on the physical well-being also and can be the causes of ulcers, etc.

God created the human body to function properly; be free from disease, and in accord with His creation. He has given His written word that we might know His laws and His will. It is the devil who has come to rob man of his birthright but Jesus overcame the devil for us.

- **1 Pet. 2:24**- *Who his own self bare our sins in his own body on the tree, that we, being dead to sins, should live unto righteousness: by whose stripes ye were healed.*

Healing is usually associated with the physical body but the INNER PERSON can be hurt in many ways and also needs healing. Being REJECTED can inflict deep wounds that last for years, even a lifetime. Rejection by a parent, a sibling, a friend, a teacher, fellow student (s), or worker (s) to be turned down for a promotion, the unfaithfulness or abandonment of a spouse can result in bitterness, anger, fear and doubt and open the door to physical illness.

The only answer is to look to Jesus as He, Himself, the only begotten Son of God, was the most rejected of all. (Isa. 53:3). From His lowly birth (in a stable) to His death on a cross, He knew rejection His earthly family, friends, the world He had come to save and even when dying He cried, "My God, My God, why hast Thou forsaken me?" (Matt. 27:46). All this He experienced for you that you can be comforted and can have a friend in every circumstance for He gives His promise:

- **<u>Heb. 13:5</u>**- *Let your conversation be without covetousness; and be content with such things as ye have: for he hath said, I will never leave thee, nor forsake thee.*

King David wrote: "When my father and my mother forsake me, then the Lord will take me up." (Psa. 27:20, 27:1).

One the cross Jesus prayed: "Father, forgive them for they know not what they do." (Luke 23:34). He requires us to forgive those who have hurt us. "Love your enemies, bless them that curse you, do good to them that hate you and pray for them that despitefully use you." *Matt. 5:44). For only as we FORGIVE are we FORGIVEN and receive His HEALING (Matt. 6:14).

This same answer is for those who have been ABUSED. With the Bible and Christian principles being ABANDONED, there are no restraints and ABUSERS are EVERYWHERE - in the home, the school, the church, the park. Little children, as well as adults, should be taught GOD'S instructions: *"CALL UPON ME in the day of trouble; I WILL DELIVER YOU and you shall GLORIFY ME."* (**<u>Psa. 50:15</u>**).

(PRAYER) DEAR JESUS, I am sorry for all my sins and by faith I receive your forgiveness and cleansing. Thou art my Lord and Savior and Deliverer even from anything that I might have inherited through family genes. I didn't realize that You can bring victory out of any circumstance and "make all things work together for my good" and bring glory to You. I forgive those who have hurt me, abused or rejected me and I pray for them. Please BLOT OUT all MEMORIES of evil words and actions. Thank You that I can now look forward to living forever where there is only true love, peace, and joy. I love you, Jesus, and thank You God, for allowing me to be in Your family...AMEN.

- **Phil. 3:13**- *Brethren, I count not myself to have apprehended: but this one thing I do, forgetting those things which are behind, and reaching forth unto those things which are before,*

("I'm sorry", "Forgive me", "I forgive you", "I love you" are healing words. Use them.)

<u>HOLINESS</u>

SANCTIFY believer means is "to set apart for sacred use." The believer is "sanctified" through the work of the SPIRIT (1 Pet. 1:2) and through reading and obedience of the word. "*Sanctify them through thy truth: thy word is truth.*" (<u>**John 17:17**</u>).

- <u>**1 Thess. 5:23**</u>- *And the very God of peace sanctify you wholly; and I pray God your whole spirit and soul and body be preserved blameless unto the coming of our Lord Jesus Christ.*

- <u>**Col. 3:2**</u>- *Set your affection on things above, not on things on the earth.*

- <u>**Col. 3:17**</u>- *And whatsoever ye do in word or deed, do all in the name of the Lord Jesus, giving thanks to God and the Father by him.*

- <u>**1 Cor. 10:31**</u>- *Whether therefore ye eat, or*

drink, or whatsoever ye do, do all to the glory of God.

- **James 1:27**- *Pure religion and undefiled before God and the Father is this, To visit the fatherless and widows in their affliction, and to keep himself unspotted from the world.*

- **1 John 2:6**- *He that saith he abideth in him ought himself also so to walk, even as he walked.*

- **2 Cor. 7:1**- *Having therefore these promises, dearly beloved, let us cleanse ourselves from all filthiness of the flesh and spirit, perfecting holiness in the fear of God.*

- **Rom. 12:1-2**- *I beseech you therefore, brethren, by the mercies of God, that ye present your bodies a living sacrifice, holy, acceptable unto God, which is your reasonable service. [2] And be not conformed to this world: but be ye transformed by the renewing of your mind, that ye may prove what is that good, and acceptable, and perfect, will of God.*

- **1 Pet. 1:15-16**- *But as he which hath called you is holy, so be ye holy in all manner of conversation; [16] Because it is written, Be ye holy; for I am holy.*

- **Heb. 12:6**- *For whom the Lord loveth he chasteneth, and scourgeth every son whom he receiveth.*

- **Heb. 12:10**- *For they verily for a few days chastened us after their own pleasure; but he for our profit, that we might be partakers of his holiness.*

- **<u>Heb. 12:14</u>**- *Follow peace with all men, and holiness, without which no man shall see the Lord:*

HOLY SPIRIT

Who is the Holy Spirit?

The HOLY SPIRIT is the EXECUTOR-CONSUMATOR of the Godhead: The COMFORTER and ETERNAL SPIRIT. He is omnipotent, omniscient and omnipresent. The human body is His temple but He must be in-vited to indwell. He can be resisted, (Acts 7: 51) grieved , (Eph. 4: 30) quenched, (1 Thess. 5: 19) can depart,(1 Sam.16:14) and can be sinned against. (Mat.12:31,32).

GOD is the SOURCE of ALL POWER and ALL THINGS.

JESUS is the WORD, the WISDOM and the POWER of GOD and ONLY WAY to HIM.

HOLY SPIRIT is the POWER LINE. He:

- Creates
- Renews
- Convicts of sin
- Baptizes
- Guides

- Anoints
- Empowers
- Sanctifies
- Bears witness
- Reveals things of

God
- Comforts
- Gives joy
- Gives discernment
- Bears fruit
- Gives gifts
- Speaks
- Teaches
- Makes intercession
- Illuminates the mind

- **John 3:5**- *Jesus answered, Verily, verily, I say unto thee, Except a man be born of water and of the Spirit, he cannot enter into the kingdom of God.*

The HOLY SPIRIT is to lead the child of God into all truth. He shows how the Holy Word ap-plies to daily living. He makes Jesus a living and breathing reality every minute and hour of the day. (The third dimension!) without Him, man is unable to accomplish God's eternal purpose for him.

As the darkness thickens, man will not be able to stand or survive without the Holy Comforter. He will not be able to overcome and conquer without the fullness, the overflow and the edification of the Spirit. Jesus is at the right hand of the Father, waiting to shed forth His great gift for His bride, the Baptism of the Holy Spirit for the power, love and boldness to accomplish the Father's will.

As Abraham's servant brought gifts from Isaac to Rebecca before he took her back to meet Isaac; the Holy Spirit has came to seek the bride, give her gifts and take her to meet the HEAVENLY BRIDEGROOM in the air!

- **Rev. 22:17**- *And the Spirit and the Bride say "Come."*

The Holy Spirit Through the Bible

GOD, by one name or another, is acknowledged throughout the world but "no man hath seen God at any time."

- **Ex. 33:20**- *And he said, Thou canst not see my face: for there shall no man see me, and live.*

GOD THE SON (Jesus in His preincarnate form) was seen in person by such as Abraham, Isaac, Jacob, Moses, et al. and He "was made flesh and dwelt among us," but GOD THE HOLY SPIRIT, although mentioned from the first chapter of the Bible to the last one, is virtually unknown to most people. They have not recognized that it was He (the voice of conscience) that made them feel bad or want to hide after having done something that was contrary to God's will. After being continually ignored, however, He will quit speaking.

- **Gen. 6:3**- *And the LORD said, My spirit shall not always strive with man, for that he also is flesh: yet his days shall be an hundred and twenty years.*

The Holy Spirit is a personality, for Jesus referred to 'him or 'he" when speaking of the Spirit yet He has NO BODY as He is omnipresent. The Greek name for the

Holy Spirit is *"Hagios pneuma."* (Holy Wind, lit. trans.) and wind cannot be present without moving something or being felt.

- **Gen. 1:2**- *And the earth was without form, and void; and darkness was upon the face of the deep. And the Spirit of God moved upon the face of the waters.*
- **Zech. 4:6**- *Then he answered and spake unto me, saying, This is the word of the LORD unto Zerubbabel, saying, Not by might, nor by power, but by my spirit, saith the LORD of hosts.*

To be equated with, but greater than, might and power indicates that one of the Spirit's at-tributes is POWER in the SUPERLATIVE degree, or SUPERnatural.

For the special task of making the Tabernacle in the wilderness, where God would be worship-ped: Moses said:

- **Ex. 35:31**- *And he hath filled him with the spirit of God, in wisdom, in understanding, and in knowledge, and in all manner of workmanship;*

The Spirit was on Joshua so that by faith he commanded the work of God's hands: *"Concerning the work of my hands command ye me."* (**Isa. 45:11**).

- **Deut. 34:9**- *And Joshua the son of Nun was full of the spirit of wisdom; for Moses had laid his hands upon him: and the children of Israel hearkened unto him, and did as* *the LORD commanded Moses.*

- **Jos. 10:12-13**- *Then spake Joshua to the LORD in the day when the LORD delivered up the Amorites before the children of Israel, and he said in the sight of Israel, Sun, stand thou still upon Gibeon; and thou, Moon, in the valley of Ajalon. [13] And the sun stood still, and the moon stayed, until the people had avenged themselves upon their enemies. Is not this written in the book of Jasher? So the sun stood still in the midst of heaven, and hasted not to go down about a whole day.*

Joseph was able to supernaturally interpret dreams and even Pharaoh recognized the source of his knowledge:

- **Gen. 41:38**- *And Pharaoh said unto his servants, Can we find such a one as this is, a man in whom the Spirit of God is?*

Hundreds of years later, King Nebuchadnezzar recognized the same source in Daniel.

- **Dan. 4:18**- *This dream I king Nebuchadnezzar have seen. Now thou, O Belteshazzar, declare the interpretation thereof, forasmuch as all the wise men of my kingdom are not able to make known unto me the interpretation: but thou art able; for the spirit of the holy gods is in thee.*

The outstanding judges of Israel were Othniel: Deborah, the prophetess; Gideon; Jepthah and Sampson; all of whom the Bible states: "And the Spirit of the Lord capon him."

- **Micah 3:8**- *But truly I am full of power by the spirit of the LORD, and of judgment, and of might, to declare unto Jacob his transgression, and to Israel his sin.*

****

The Holy Spirit has no voice yet Jesus said:

- **John 16:13**- *Howbeit when he, the Spirit of truth, is come, he will guide you into all truth: for he shall not speak of himself; but whatsoever he shall hear, that shall he speak: and he will shew you things to come.*

PROPHECY is inspired utterance - the DIRECT WORDS of GOD spoken by the Holy Spirit. Using the human mouth.

- **Num. 11:25-26**- *And the LORD came down in a cloud, and spake unto him, and took of the spirit that was upon him, and gave it unto the seventy elders: and it came to pass, that, when the spirit rested upon them, they prophesied, and did not cease. [26] But there remained two of the men in the camp, the name of the one was Eldad, and the name of the other Medad: and the spirit rested upon them; and they were of them that were written, but went not out unto the tabernacle: and they prophesied in the camp.*
- **1 Sam. 10:10**- *And when they came thither to the hill, behold, a company of prophets met him; and the Spirit of God came upon him, and he*

prophesied among them.

- **Acts 1:16**- *Men and brethren, this scripture must needs have been fulfilled, which the Holy Ghost by the mouth of David spake before concerning Judas, which was guide to them that took Jesus.*

- **Jer. 36:4**- *Then Jeremiah called Baruch the son of Neriah: and Baruch wrote from the mouth of Jeremiah all the words of the LORD, which he had spoken unto him, upon a roll of a book.*

- **Ezek. 11:5**- *And the Spirit of the LORD fell upon me, and said unto me, Speak; Thus saith the LORD; Thus have ye said, O house of Israel: for I know the things that come into your mind, every one of them.*

God's word has a silence of 400 years with apparently no inspired revelation to His people. Then an angel was sent to the priest Zacharias to announce the birth of his son, John the Baptist:

- **Luke 1:15**- *For he shall be great in the sight of the Lord, and shall drink neither wine nor strong drink; and he shall be filled with the Holy Ghost, even from his mother's womb.*

- **Luke 1:41**- *And it came to pass, that, when Elisabeth heard the salutation of Mary, the babe leaped in her womb; and Elisabeth was filled with the Holy Ghost:*

At the birth of John, "Zacharias was filled with the Holy Ghost" and "prophesied." Thus the entire family was willed with the Holy Ghost. When the child Jesus was taken to the temple; Simeon a just and devout man, "came by the Spirit into the temple," for "the HOLY GHJOST was upon him." He took Jesus in his arms and prophesied; and "*Anna, a prophetess, gave thanks likewise.*" Although these five are mentioned in the New Testament, they are the last to have the Holy Spirit upon them in the Old Testament manner; only by God's choosing and only for special tasks or occasions. The Spirit's power on these people was sufficient to influence all Israel for God and at their passing, spiritual disaster ensued until God raised up another.

John the Baptist said TWO things about Jesus:

- **John 1:29**- *The next day John seeth Jesus coming unto him, and saith, Behold the Lamb of God, which taketh away the sin of the world.*
- **Luke 3:16**- *John answered, saying unto them all, I indeed baptize you with water; but one mightier than I cometh, the latchet of whose shoes I am not worthy to unloose: he shall baptize you with the Holy Ghost and with fire.*

The first statement is mentioned ONLY in one gospel, whereas the second is in ALL FOUR GOSPELS, emphasizing the great importance of this aspect of His coming which could not be fulfilled until He had ascended.

- **John 7:38**- *He that believeth on me, as the scripture hath said, out of his belly shall flow rivers of living water.*

- **John 14:16-17**- *And I will pray the Father, and he shall give you another Comforter, that he may abide with you for ever; [17] Even the Spirit of truth; whom the world cannot receive, because it seeth him not, neither knoweth him: but ye know him; for he dwelleth with you, and shall be in you.*

The Holy Spirit is WITH the believer for He convicts the sinner and draws him to the Lord. Upon the person's acceptance of Jesus as Savior, the Spirit invisibly baptizes him into the body of Christ at which time he is born of the Spirit.

- **1 Cor. 12:13**- *For by one Spirit are we all baptized into one body, whether we be Jews or Gentiles, whether we be bond or free; and have been all made to drink into one Spirit.*
- **Eph. 4:4-5**- *There is one body, and one Spirit, even as ye are called in one hope of your calling; [5] One Lord, one faith, one baptism,*

This is NOT the baptism that John the Baptist spoke about for JESUS was to be the BAPTIZER WITH the Holy Spirit and Jesus Himself used "that term:

- **Acts 1:5**- *For John truly baptized with water; but ye shall be baptized with the Holy Ghost not many days hence.*

Jesus was not referring to salvation nor even to its completion for He had already said to Peter; "Ye are clean." (John 13:10); and also, "Rejoice not that the spirits are subject to you, but rather rejoice, because your names are written in heaven." (Luke 10:20).

Christ's LAST and most IMPORTANT
INSTRUCTIONS to His followers were:

- **Acts 1:4**- *And, being assembled together with them, commanded them that they should not depart from Jerusalem, but wait for the promise of the Father, which, saith he, ye have heard of me.*

- **Joel 2:28-29**- *And it shall come to pass afterward, that I will pour out my spirit upon all flesh; and your sons and your daughters shall prophesy, your old men shall dream dreams, your young men shall see visions: [29] And also upon the servants and upon the handmaids in those days will I pour out my spirit.*

- **Acts 1:8**- *But ye shall receive power, after that the Holy Ghost is come upon you: and ye shall be witnesses unto me both in Jerusalem, and in all Judaea, and in Samaria, and unto the uttermost part of the earth.*

He did not tell them how long to wait, nor un-til the Day of Pentecost, nor how they would know they had been baptized. If they could have taken it by faith they need not have waited ten days.

- **Acts 2:1-4**- *And when the day of Pentecost was fully come, they were all with one accord in one place. [2] And suddenly there came a sound from heaven as of a rushing mighty wind, and it filled all the house where they were sitting. [3] And there*

> *appeared unto them cloven tongues like as of fire, and it sat upon each of them. 4 And they were all filled with the Holy Ghost, and began to speak with other tongues, as the Spirit gave them utterance.*

Only at this initial outpouring of the Holy Spirit was there a period of tarrying, the sound of wind and the cloven tongues of fire. However, the speaking in tongues was always thereafter mentioned or implied in subsequent experiences recorded in Acts. Just as in the Old Testament, the Holy Spirit USED THE MOUTH to indicate His presence and to again be the means of God speaking to His people.

The "speaking in tongues" had a 4-fold purpose:

1. To control the whole person:
   - **James 3:8**- *But the tongue can no man tame; it is an unruly evil, full of deadly poison.*

   As "bits are put into horses' mouths, that they may obey us," the Spirit controlling the tongue to the extent of using it to speak an unlearned language, certainly in-dicates complete surrender. Jesus did not speak in tongues at His bap-tism because He is the author of languages and His tongue was never unruly.
   - **John 8:28**- *Then said Jesus unto them, When ye have lifted up the Son of man, then shall ye know that I am he, and that I do nothing of myself; but as my Father hath taught me, I speak these things.*

2. For a sign:
    - **1 Cor. 14:22**- *Wherefore tongues are for a sign, not to them that believe, but to them that believe not: but prophesying serveth not for them that believe not, but for them which believe.*

NO MULTITUDE came to hear the preaching of the gospel UNTIL it "*was noised abroad*" about the TONGUES.

    - **Acts 2:8-11**- *And how hear we every man in our own tongue, wherein we were born? ⁹Parthians, and Medes, and Elamites, and the dwellers in Mesopotamia, and in Judaea, and Cappadocia, in Pontus, and Asia, ¹⁰Phrygia, and Pamphylia, in Egypt, and in the parts of Libya about Cyrene, and strangers of Rome, Jews and proselytes, ¹¹Cretes and Arabians, we do hear them speak in our tongues the wonderful works of God.*

3. To Speak to God
    It is not mentioned that they ALL spoke in known tongues or that they spoke in known tongues all of the time or just when the crowd gathered for Paul wrote by the Spirit:
    - **1 Cor. 14:2**- *For he that speaketh in an unknown tongue speaketh not unto men, but unto God: for no man understandeth*

*him; howbeit in the spirit he speaketh
mysteries.*

There is NO WAY that "SPEAKING UNTO GOD"
could be wrong, or evil or from the devil! Jesus is the
Baptizer, thus "speaking in tongues" was His choosing,
not man's, and to reject or despise this is to reject and
despise Christ's gift for His bride. The Holy Spirit had
used the human mouth to speak through during the Old
Testament period in the language of the people - God
speaking to men; this is the spirit in the individual
speaking to God.

He is the author of language, not the devil. He gave
Adam a language; He separated the people by confusing
the tongues at Babel; at Pentecost He united the people
again with tongues and He will give every inhabitant of
heaven a new language that will be spok-en and
understood by all immediately.

    4. Edification
- **1 Cor. 14:4**- *He that speaketh in an
  unknown tongue edifieth himself; but he
  that prophesieth edifieth the church.*

All machinery needs maintenance; neglect it and trouble
results. God's child is surrounded by sin, sinners,
temptations, trials, and the fiery darts of the wicked one -
all working to pull him down.

Therefore, the Manufacturer's Maintenance Instructions
for the building up (renewing) of the most marvelous
piece of machinery known to man – the human body and

mind – should be followed.

Paul said, "I thank my God, I speak with tongues more than ye all:" and he withstood the most persecution (2 Cor. 12:10) and had the greatest anointing of the Holy Spirit.

Peter, who had thrice denied (with oaths) e-ven knowing Jesus, boldly proclaimed:

- **Acts 2:16-18**- *But this is that which was spoken by the prophet Joel; [17] And it shall come to pass in the last days, saith God, I will pour out of my Spirit upon all flesh: and your sons and your daughters shall prophesy, and your young men shall see visions, and your old men shall dream dreams: [18] And on my servants and on my handmaidens I will pour out in those days of my Spirit; and they shall prophesy:*
- **Acts 2:33**- *Therefore being by the right hand of God exalted, and having received of the Father the promise of the Holy Ghost, he hath shed forth this, which ye now see and hear.*

What they SAW was the joy of the "rivers of living water" flowing from their innermost being; so that they appeared as "drunken." What they heard was the "speaking in tongues the wonderful works of God."

- **Acts 2:41, 43**- *Then they that gladly received his word were baptized: and* *the same day there were added unto them about three thousand souls. 43 And fear came upon every soul: and many wonders and signs were done by the apostles.*

THERE WAS NO DOUBT but that the HOLY GHOST and FIRE had entered and was empowering the disciples -establishing the pattern for all of Christ's disciples, "even as many as the Lord our God shall call." Fire always changes the object that is burning and always affects everything it gets close to or touches.

- **Acts 17:6**- *And when they found them not, they drew Jason and certain brethren unto the rulers of the city, crying, These that have turned the world upside down are come hither also;*
- **Matt. 10:7-8**- *And as ye go, preach, saying, The kingdom of heaven is at hand. 8 Heal the sick, cleanse the lepers, raise the dead, cast out devils: freely ye have received, freely give.*
- **1 Cor. 2:4**- *And my speech and my preaching was not with enticing words of man's wisdom, but in demonstration of the Spirit and of power:*
- **Rom. 8:14**- *For as many as are led by the Spirit of God, they are the sons of God.*

It is through the power of the Holy Spirit that the

believer becomes "conformed to the image of Jesus (Rom. 8:29). For, "when He shall appear, we shall be like Him. (1 John 3:2-3).

- **Gal. 5:17; 24**- *For the flesh lusteth against the Spirit, and the Spirit against the flesh: and these are contrary the one to the other: so that ye cannot do the things that ye would. ²⁴ And they that are Christ's have crucified the flesh with the affections and lusts.*

Only a FEW are willing to pay this price and the rest will lack the power of the Spirit to stand in the evil day and will be (are being) deceived as Satan is ever present, offering to satisfy the "lust pf the eye, the lust of the flesh, and the pride of life," and give a false religious experience. Forecasters of horoscopes, psychic readers, fortune tellers, etc. are busy giving guidance, assurance of popularity, pleasures and possessions and thereby enticing the gullible, both young and old, into his web.

GOD ALONE (not stars, cards, tea leaves or humans) knows the individual - even from before conception - and because of His love, has promised to send the Holy Spirit to guide each through this life and to a wonderful, exciting "forever" with Him.

- **Psa. 1:1**- *Blessed is the man that walketh not in the counsel of the ungodly, nor standeth in the way of sinners, nor sitteth in the seat of the scornful.*
- **Rev. 2:7, 17, 29**- *He that hath an ear, let him hear what the Spirit saith unto the churches; To*

him that overcometh will I give to eat of the tree of life, which is in the midst of the paradise of God. [17] He that hath an ear, let him hear what the Spirit saith unto the churches; To him that overcometh will I give to eat of the hidden manna, and will give him a white stone, and in the stone a new name written, which no man knoweth saving he that receiveth it. [29] He that hath an ear, let him hear what the Spirit saith unto the churches.

- **Rev. 3:6, 13, 22**- *He that hath an ear, let him hear what the Spirit saith unto the churches. [13] He that hath an ear, let him hear what the Spirit saith unto the churches. [22] He that hath an ear, let him hear what the Spirit saith unto the churches.*

Like the servant who sought and brought a bride to Abraham's son Isaac, the Holy Spirit is seeking, powering, and unifying Christ's bride.

LOVE is not the only binding force, as many are now proclaiming, for the "fellowship of the Spirit" includes being "like minded," "of one accord," "honest" and believing the same core truths of the faith.

The Holy Spirit does not teach opposing beliefs or doctrines to different members or groups within the Bride. If all are truly hearing and following the voice and leading of the Spirit in sincere humility, there will be unity.

- **Psa. 119:4**- *Thou hast commanded us to keep*

thy precepts diligently

- **1 John 1:7-8**- *But if we walk in the light, as he is in the light, we have fellowship one with another, and the blood of Jesus Christ his Son cleanseth us from all sin. ⁸ If we say that we have no sin, we deceive ourselves, and the truth is not in us.*

Remember these important instructions: "BE NOT DECEIVED," and "WALK IN THE SPIRIT."

Baptism (Gifts)

As with counselling or assisting inquirers to receive salvation, it is in order to encourage people to receive the baptism.

- **Acts 8:14-17**- *Now when the apostles which were at Jerusalem heard that Samaria had received the word of God, they sent unto them Peter and John: ¹⁵ Who, when they were come down, prayed for them, that they might receive the Holy Ghost: ¹⁶ (For as yet he was fallen upon none of them: only they were baptized in the name of the Lord Jesus.) ¹⁷ Then laid they their hands on them, and they received the Holy Ghost.*

There are two basic requirements:

1. **Acts 5:32**- *We are his witnesses of these things; and so is also the Holy Ghost, whom God hath given to them that OBEY HIM.*

Obedience is knowing Jesus as Savior and having also presented your body as a living sacrifice, HOLY, and acceptable unto God for the Holy Spirit is going to move from being "with you" to being "in you." Know ye not that your body is the temple of the Holy Ghost?"

2. **Luke 11:11-13**- *If a son shall ask bread of any of you that is a father, will he give him a stone? or if he ask a fish, will he for a fish give him a serpent? [12] Or if he shall ask an egg, will he offer him a scorpion? [13] If ye then, being evil, know how to give good gifts unto your children: how much more shall your heavenly Father give the Holy Spirit to them that ask him?*

Salvation is for all but only those who repent, confess and receive are saved. The promise of the Holy Ghost is "for all flesh" but the individual must ask, yield and receive. Peter not only asked to walk on the water, but of his run free will got out of the boat and moved his legs in a walking motion and he received the water made firm. The other disciples were in the boat; they did not ask -nor did they try, nor did they walk.

(Suggested Prayer)

Dear Jesus, I trust You as my Lord and Savior, but anything in my life that is displeasing to You I now surrender and ask to be cleansed by Your blood which I also claim as protection against the evil one. I give myself to You -body, soul and spirit -for You to control. Baptize me with Your Holy Spirit; use me in Your service. Help me to always glorify Your name. AMEN.

Continue in a praising, prayerful and expectant attitude. Jesus "breathed on them, and saith unto them, Receive ye the HolyGhost; so breathe in the Holy Spirit for "out of your innermost being shall flow rivers of living water." As it is humanly impossible to speak two languages at the same time; stop speaking in your own, and by faith make a sound, ("*Make a joyful unto the Lord*" (Psa. 98:4)) and as Peter by faith walked, by faith speak and Jesus will give you the new, clean, undefiled language with which yourspir1t may commune with Him. Jesus will NOT FORCE you to speak, any more than He forced Peter to walk. Although Peter walked on the water, he became afraid and began to sink. After you have received, do not let the devil cause you to fear or doubt. This is not an intellectual experience, but a spiritual one -a liberation -an abandonment you have not known before.

- **<u>Rom. 8:26-27</u>**- *Likewise the Spirit also helpeth our infirmities: for we know not what we should pray for as we ought: but the Spirit itself maketh intercession for us with groanings which cannot be uttered. [27] And he that searcheth the hearts knoweth what is the mind of the Spirit, because he maketh intercession for the saints according to the will of God.*

Daily follow Paul's pattern; "I will pray with the Spirit and I will pray with the understanding also: I will sing with the spirit, and I will sing with the understanding also."

Most people after receiving, have a new sense of appreciation of God's marvelous creation (the sky bluer and the grass greener) and have a feeling of love as never before. Most of all, Jesus becomes a living personality and His word a new and fascinating book.

You will want to share your experience but don't be discouraged if others are not so enthusiastic. If a person hasn't received salvation he will hardly understand a deeper experience. If you meet with strong opposition, graciously warn that ATTRIBUTING the WORKS of the HOLY SPIRIT to the devil is the UNPARDONABLE SIN.

- **Matt. 12:32**- *And whosoever speaketh a word against the Son of man, it shall be forgiven him: but whosoever speaketh against the Holy Ghost, it shall not be forgiven him, neither in this world, neither in the world to come.*

Results of the Baptism
(Fruits and Gifts of the Spirit)

When Jesus returned to the Father He commissioned His followers to carry on His ministry in the SAME MANNER and POWER AS HE HAD.

- **John 20:21**- *Then said Jesus to them again, Peace be unto you: as my Father hath sent me, even so send I you.*

- **John 14:12**- *Verily, verily, I say unto you, He that believeth on me, the works that I do shall he do also; and greater works than these shall he do; because I go unto my Father.*

- **Acts 1:8**- *But ye shall receive power, after that the Holy Ghost is come upon you: and ye shall be witnesses unto me both in Jerusalem, and in all Judaea, and in Samaria, and unto the uttermost part of the earth.*

- **Acts 5:12**- *And by the hands of the apostles were many signs and wonders wrought among the people; (and they were all with one accord in Solomon's porch.*

- **Mark 16:17-18**- *And these signs shall follow them that believe; In my name shall they cast out devils; they shall speak with new tongues; [18] They shall take up serpents; and if they drink any deadly thing, it shall not hurt them; they shall lay hands on the sick, and they shall recover.*

These are the credentials of ALL BELIEVERS in ALL PLACES, and for ALL TIMES. As with all of God's promises, they must be appropriated by the individual.

****

SPIRITUAL FRUIT, like the natural, develop over a period of time.

- **Gal. 5:22**- *But the fruit of the Spirit is love, joy, peace, longsuffering, gentleness, goodness, faith,*

The GIFTS OF THE SPIRIT do not grow on a Christian, but are given by the Spirit.

- **1 Cor. 12:4-12**- *Now there are diversities of gifts, but the same Spirit. [5] And there are differences of administrations, but the same Lord. [6] And there are diversities of operations, but it is the same God which worketh all in all. [7] But the manifestation of the Spirit is given to every man to profit withal. [8] For to one is given by the Spirit the word of wisdom; to another the word of knowledge by the same Spirit; [9] To another faith by the same Spirit; to another the gifts of healing by the same Spirit; [10] To another the working of miracles; to another prophecy; to another discerning of spirits; to another divers kinds of tongues; to another the interpretation of tongues: [11] But all these worketh that one and the selfsame Spirit, dividing to every man severally as he will. [12] For as the body is one, and hath many members, and all the members of that one body, being many, are one body: so also is Christ.*

WISDOM- God- given spiritual perception

KNOWLEDGE- supernatural revelation of that which could not be known otherwise.

FAITH- supernatural confidence in God's ability

GIFTS OF HEALING- special God- given faith for raising up of the sick

WORKING OF MIRACLES- supernatural acts performed by God's power working through the believer

PROPHECY- God speaking through the human mouth in supernatural utterance for the edification, exhortation, and comfort of His children as well as foretelling coming judgment or future events.

DISCERNING OF SPIRITS- the supernatural ability to detect the presence of a demonic spirit.

DIVERS KINDS OF TONGUES- the supernatural ability to speak in a language known to the hearer but unknown not to the speaker; also, to speak of supernatural interpretation by the speaker himself or by another. (This is not to be confused with the evidence of the baptism or the prayer language wherein a person speaks unto God. This has been greatly misunderstood because Paul asked: "Are all prophets?... do all speak with tongues? Do all interpret?" The obvious answer is "No" as these are SPECIAL GIFTS for USE IN THE BODY for God to speak to His people.

INTERPRETATION OF TONGUES - the God-given ability (not to understand but) to supernaturally utter the translation in the language of the hearers of that which has been said in the unknown tongue

Prophecy is for believers – they recognize when God is speaking. Tongues and interpretation equals prophecy but the tongues "are for a sign to the unbeliever." That he might be alerted to hear what God has to say. (1 Cor. 14:5).

- **<u>John 16:13</u>**- *Howbeit when he, the Spirit of truth, is come, he will guide you into all truth: for he shall not speak of himself; but whatsoever he shall hear, that shall he speak: and he will shew you things to come.*

- **<u>1 Thess. 5:19-20</u>**- *Quench not the Spirit. [20] Despise not prophesyings.*

- **<u>1 Cor. 14:26, 40</u>**- *How is it then, brethren? when ye come together, every one of you hath a psalm, hath a doctrine, hath a tongue, hath a revelation, hath an interpretation. Let all things be done unto edifying. [40] Let all things be done decently and in order.*

JEWS

God's Redemptive Plan for the World
The Scriptures start with "In the beginning God "Created." (Actually "God" as *Elohim* is plural but "Created" is singular. Verse 2 declares: "The Spirit of God moved... (*Ruach Elohim*). Verse 26: "And God said, Let US make man in OUR image. After OUR likeness." To whom is God speaking who has the SAME IMAGE and LIKENESS as He and who has the POWER TO CREATE WITH Him?

- **Psa. 2:7**- *I will declare the decree: the LORD hath said unto me, Thou art my Son; this day have I begotten thee.*
- **Prov. 8:22-31**- *The LORD possessed me in the beginning of his way, before his works of old.*

²³ I was set up from everlasting, from the beginning, or ever the earth was. ²⁴ When there were no depths, I was brought forth; when there were no fountains abounding with water. ²⁵ Before the mountains were settled, before the hills was I brought forth: ²⁶ While as yet he had not made the earth, nor the fields, nor the highest part of the dust of the world. ²⁷ When he prepared the heavens, I was there: when he set a compass upon the face of the depth: ²⁸ When he established the clouds above: when he strengthened the fountains of the deep: ²⁹ When he gave to the sea his decree, that the waters should not pass his commandment: when he appointed the foundations of the earth: ³⁰ Then I was by him, as one brought up with him: and I was daily his delight, rejoicing always before him; ³¹ Rejoicing in the habitable part of his earth; and my delights were with the sons of men.

- **John 1:1-3**- *In the beginning was the Word, and the Word was with God, and the Word was God. ² The same was in the beginning with God. ³ All things were made by him; and without him was not any thing made that was made.*

All things were made by Him: and without Him was not anything made that was made. (Who is the Word? "The Word was made flesh, and dwelt among us." Therefore, the Word can be none other than Jesus.

How can this be reconciled with the "*Shema*?"

- **Deut. 6:4**- *Hear, O Israel: The LORD our God is one LORD:*

The word "one" is "*echod*" which means "a composite

one, not "*yachid*" a singular one, which is never used with the Godhead in Scriptures. (See "You Shall Know the Truth" at the front of this book).

Thus, when Isaiah wrote: "Holy, holy, holy is the Lord of hosts," he was describing each member of the Triune Godhead.

GOD IS HOLY and when Adam and Eve sinned, their fellowship with Him was broken and His law- "without the shedding of blood there is no remission of sins," had to be satisfied. Thus, God Himself, killed an innocent animal – the FIRST SHEDDING OF BLOOD -- and made coats of skin and clothed them. (Gen. 3:21). However, Adam "brought forth after his kind" and the world became populated with "sinners" whose sins were covered by the blood of animals, looking forward to the offering of a perfect sacrifice that would once and for all satisfy the broken law.

- **Rom. 5:19**- *For as by one man's disobedience many were made sinners, so by the obedience of one shall many be made righteous.*

After the Flood, the world was again populated with sinners. There is not, nor has been a per-son who is not a descendent of one of Noah's three sons - Shem, Ham and Japheth; which ac-counts for the varied stories of the Flood found in the ruins of ancient civilizations a-round the world; along with altars on which blood sacrifices were offered, and indications of a belief in a life after death.

God's laws have to be kept or the penalty for breaking them has to be paid. God knew man could never do either one. As He saved Noah and his family in the Ark from the Flood, God had a plan whereby all the nations of the world might be saved as well as having His justice upheld and His broken laws satisfied. Of the 3 sons of Noah, He selected the family of Shem to bring salvation to the descendants of ALL the children of Noah. Thus it was that Abraham was called:

- **<u>Gen. 12:2-3</u>**- *And I will make of thee a great nation, and I will bless thee, and make thy name great; and thou shalt be a blessing: [3] And I will bless them that bless thee, and curse him that curseth thee: and in thee shall all families of the earth be blessed.*

As God had started with Adam and his family; then started over with Noah and his family; now Abraham and his selected line of descendants would' be God's "chosen people." Few realize that Abraham was not a Jew, nor was Isaac, nor Jacob; nor were Abraham and Isaac - Israelites. They were "Semites" (descendants of Shem) and were also called Hebrews. ("One from the other side of the river." lit.trans.)

Abraham's first son was Ishmael (the father of all Arabs) but the selection was in Isaac; (son of Sarah, a Semite) Isaac's son Esau was the "father of the Edomites in mount Seir" but his twin, Jacob, was the chosen one. After a night of wrestling with God, his name was changed from Jacob (supplanter) to Israel (who pre-vails with God),and his 12 sons became the 12 tribes of Israel.

The designation of "Jew" came later, referring to members of the houses of Judah and Benjamin, the "Southern Kingdom" when the division came after Solomon's reign.

The entire Old Testament is the account of God's dealing with His chosen people; bringing to them and through them graphic, unmistakable illustrations of His plan for the redemption of not only their nation, but for the WORLD THROUGH THEM.

Abraham had no law, nor did Isaac, Jacob or Joseph, nor the children of Israel for 400 yrs. in Egypt.

- **Rom. 4:3**- *For what saith the scripture? Abraham believed God, and it was counted unto him for righteousness.*
- **Rom. 3:28**- *Therefore we conclude that a man is justified by faith without the deeds of the law.*
- **Rom. 3:23**- *For all have sinned, and come short of the glory of God;*

When Abraham was ascending Mt. Moriah to sacrifice his beloved son, he did not realize he was actually stating God's redemptive plan FOR THE WORLD when he said: "God will PROVIDE HIMSELF a LAMB for a burnt offering."

Nearly, 2,000 years later on the night commemorating the slaying of the First Passover Lamb, God led His beloved Son to almost the exact spot where Isaac had been laid on the altar. The hands and feet of God's Son were not bound, though; they were cruelly pierced with nails. Abraham's lifted hand was stayed by an angel so that he did not have to slay the son of promise for whom he had waited so long.

Jesus was also the Son of Promise for whom the world had been waiting so many centuries but God could not stay His own hand for "*He was the Lamb slain from the foundation of the world.*" (**Rev. 13:8**). "*To this end was I born, and for this cause came I into the world.*" (**John 18:37**).

- **Isa. 53:3-10**- *He is despised and rejected of men; a man of sorrows, and acquainted with grief: and we hid as it were our faces from him; he was despised, and we esteemed him not. [4] Surely he hath borne our griefs, and carried our sorrows: yet we did esteem him stricken, smitten of God, and afflicted. [5] But he was wounded for our transgressions, he was bruised for our iniquities: the chastisement of our peace was upon him; and with his stripes we are healed. [6] All we like sheep have gone astray; we have turned every one to his own way; and the LORD hath laid on him the iniquity of us all. [7] He was oppressed, and he was afflicted, yet he opened not his mouth: he is brought as a lamb to the slaughter, and as a sheep before her shearers is dumb, so he openeth not his mouth. [8] He was taken from prison and from judgment: and who shall declare his generation? for he was cut off out of the land of the living: for the transgression of my people was he stricken. [9] And he made his*

grave with the wicked, and with the rich in
his death; because he had done no violence,
neither was any deceit in his mouth. [10] *Yet it*
pleased the LORD to bruise him; he hath put
him to grief: when thou shalt make his soul
an offering for sin, he shall see his seed, he
shall prolong his days, and the pleasure of
the LORD shall prosper in his hand.

How could God be pleased to bruise His beloved Son who had been with Him "or ever the earth was" who had daily been his delight, rejoicing always before Him?" How could HE turn a deaf ear to His Son's agonizing call, "My God, My God, Why hast thou forsaken Me?"

God cannot look upon sin and all the vile sins that had ever been or ever would be committed and all the sickness and disease were laid on this Innocent Lamb, *"being made a curse for us: for it is written, Cursed is every one that hangeth on a tree." "To wit, that God was in Christ reconciling the world to Himself, not imputing their trespasses unto them; For He hath made HIM TO BE SIN FOR US, who knew no sin; that we might be made the righteousness of God in Him."* (**2 Cor. 5:19-21**).

How could Jesus have willingly *"given Himself a ransom for all?"*

- **Heb. 12:2**- *Looking unto Jesus the author and finisher of our faith; who for the joy that was set before him endured the cross, despising the shame, and is set down at the right hand of the throne of God.*

- **1 Pet. 1:18-19**- *Forasmuch as ye know that ye were not redeemed with corruptible things, as silver and gold, from your vain conversation received by tradition from your fathers; [19] But with the precious blood of Christ, as of a lamb without blemish and without spot:*

The price had been paid but death had to be conquered for "If Christ be not risen, then is our preaching vain, and your faith is also vain." (1 Cor. 15:14).

- **Matt. 28:5-7**- *And the angel answered and said unto the women, Fear not ye: for I know that ye seek Jesus, which was crucified. [6] He is not here: for he is risen, as he said. Come, see the place where the Lord lay. [7] And go quickly, and tell his disciples that he is risen from the dead; and, behold, he goeth before you into Galilee; there shall ye see him: lo, I have told you.*
- **1 Cor. 15:5-6**- *And that he was seen of Cephas, then of the twelve: [6] After that, he was seen of above five hundred brethren at once; of whom the greater part remain unto this present, but some are fallen asleep.*
- **Acts 1:9-11**- *And when he had spoken these things, while they beheld, he was taken up; and a cloud received him out of their sight. [10] And while they looked stedfastly toward heaven as he went up, behold, two men stood by them in white apparel; [11] Which also said, Ye men of Galilee, why stand ye gazing up into heaven? this same Jesus, which is taken up from you into heaven, shall so come in*

like manner as ye have seen him go into heaven.

- **Heb. 9:24**- *For Christ is not entered into the holy places made with hands, which are the figures of the true; but into heaven itself, now to appear in the presence of God for us:*

- **Heb. 4:15-16**- *For we have not an high priest which cannot be touched with the feeling of our infirmities; but was in all points tempted like as we are, yet without sin. 16 Let us therefore come boldly unto the throne of grace, that we may obtain mercy, and find grace to help in time of need.*

- **Jer. 31:31**- *Behold, the days come, saith the LORD, that I will make a new covenant with the house of Israel, and with the house of Judah:*

- **Gal. 3:13**- *Christ hath redeemed us from the curse of the law, being made a curse for us: for it is written, Cursed is every one that hangeth on a tree:*

- **Isa. 49:6-7**- *And he said, It is a light thing that thou shouldest be my servant to raise up the tribes of Jacob, and to restore the preserved of Israel: I will also give thee for a light to the Gentiles, that thou mayest be my salvation unto the end of the earth. 7 Thus saith the LORD, the Redeemer of Israel, and his Holy One, to him whom man despiseth, to him whom the nation abhorreth, to a servant of rulers, Kings shall see and arise, princes also shall worship, because of the LORD that is faithful, and the Holy One of Israel, and he shall choose thee.*

Therefore, CHRISTIANITY is NOT GENTILE: it is the continuation of God's salvation for the WHOLE WORLD. All the first Christians were JEWISH. True Gentile Christians love the Jews. Through the centuries they, too, have been persecuted and murdered in like manner and in equally great numbers.

As Satan has USED LOST, UNGODLY Gentiles to persecute the Jews and commit terrible atrocities against them in the name of Christianity, he has kept the vast majority of Jews from drinking of the "Water of life" although they were the means for providing it for all people.

- **Matt. 8:11**- *And I say unto you, That many shall come from the east and west, and shall sit down with Abraham, and Isaac, and Jacob, in the kingdom of heaven.*
- **John 1:11-12**- *He came unto his own, and his own received him not. [12] But as many as received him, to them gave he power to become the sons of God, even to them that believe on his name:*
- **Prov. 30:4**- *Who hath ascended up into heaven, or descended? who hath gathered the wind in his fists? who hath bound the waters in a garment? who hath established all the ends of the earth? what is his name, and what is his son's name, if thou canst tell?*

If his name is so important, why was it not mentioned somewhere in the Scriptures? (O.T.) IT WAS! "Jesus" is

Greek; the Hebrew is "YESHUA" and it appears about 100 times all the way from Genesis to Habakkuk!

- **Isa. 62:11**- *Behold, the LORD hath proclaimed unto the end of the world, Say ye to the daughter of Zion, Behold, thy salvation cometh; behold, his reward is with him, and his work before him.*
- **Isa. 7:14**- *Therefore the Lord himself shall give you a sign; Behold, a virgin shall conceive, and bear a son, and shall call his name Immanuel.*

YESHUA is the very name that the angel Gabriel used when he told Mary about the Son she was to have, The very name the angel spoke to Joseph, espoused husband of Mary: *"And she shall bring forth a Son, and that shall call His name YESHUA (Salvation) for He shall save His people from their sins."* (**Matt. 1:21**).

- **Acts 4:12**- *Neither is there salvation in any other: for there is none other name under heaven given among men, whereby we must be saved.*

Every PASSOVER, unknowingly the death, burial and resurrection of YESHUA is commemorated. The 3 matzahs represent the *echod* (composite) *Elohim* (plural) -God the Father, God the Son and God the Holy Spirit, The middle matzah, representing the Son, is taken out and broken into TWO pieces, Jesus was the Son of God in the flesh; also the Son of Man (born of the virgin Mary). Therefore it was the man Yeshua that was broken.

- **1 Cor. 11:23-24**- *For I have received of the Lord that which also I delivered unto you, that the Lord Jesus the same night in which he was betrayed took bread: 24 And when he had given thanks, he brake it, and said, Take, eat: this is my body, which is broken for you: this do in remembrance of me.*

The piece of matzah, then wrapped in a clean cloth and hidden, represents the burial of the body of Yeshua - hidden in the grave. "When Joseph had taken the body, he wrapped it in a clean linen cloth, and laid it in his own new tomb."

The mandatory use of red wine for the celebrating of "The Seder" (a new ingredient not found in the writings of Moses) represents the blood of Jesus. "He took the cup… saying: "This is my blood of the new testament, which is shed for many for the remission of sins."

The hidden matzah is brought out again, broken and distributed to all (the "Afikomen") and no other food is taken during the remainder of the evening. This represents the resurrection, the finished work of Yeshua; nothing more needs to be added; He fulfilled all of the Law and became the Passover Lamb; but He must be taken into each life – "eaten" as it were.

- **John 6:51, 54, 58**- *I am the living bread which came down from heaven: if any man eat of this bread, he shall live for ever: and* *the bread that I will give is my flesh, which I will give for the life of the world. [54] Whoso eateth my flesh, and drinketh my blood, hath eternal life; and I will raise him up at the last day. [58] This is that bread which came down from heaven: not as your fathers did eat manna, and are dead: he that eateth of this bread shall live for ever.*

The mysterious word "*Afikomen*" is of Greek derivation and means "I CAME." Who came? The One whom the broken matzah represents - Yeshua.

- **John 3:16**- *For God so loved the world, that he gave his only begotten Son, that whosoever believeth in him should not perish, but have everlasting life.*

Shoichi Yokoi, a former Japanese Imperial Army sergeant, emerged from the jungles of a South Pacific island in 1972 after 28 years of living on fish and jungle plants; eluding capture, not knowing that World War II had ended and peace declared.

The BATTLE IS OVER for YOU! PEACE WITH GOD has been WON! As a "child of the Kingdom" of the "seed of Abraham," wait no longer to claim the atoning blood of God's Lamb, Messiah of Israel and Savior of all men.

- **Rom. 10:9**- *That if thou shalt confess with thy mouth the Lord Jesus, and shalt believe in thine heart that God hath raised him from* *the dead, thou shalt be saved.*

- **Rom. 10:12-13**- *For there is no difference between the Jew and the Greek: for the same Lord over all is rich unto all that call upon him. [13] For whosoever shall call upon the name of the Lord shall be saved.*

(Suggested Prayer)

BLESSED ART THOU. O GOD; Hear my prayer and have mercy upon me. I have tried to serve Thee according to that which I have been taught. I now realize that Yeshua (Jesus) was actually our Messiah and I claim the blood He shed on the cross as the atonement for my sins. I be-lieve He arose from the dead by Thy power. I thank Thee for Thy marvelous plan of salvation not only for my people, but for all people.

I believe Thou hast heard this prayer and hast FORGIVEN me and SAVED me. Create in me a clean heart, O God; and put a right spirit within me. Help me from this day on to live in a manner that will be pleasing to Thee and bring glory to Thy name. Open my eyes and ears of understanding of Thy word.

O God, my God, I praise Thee. Yeshua, Thou art my Savior; I thank Thee for dying for me. Holy Spirit, I acknowledge Thee although I know very little about Thee. Help me to learn more.

O Lord, as Thou didst bring our fathers from slavery to freedom; bring me to a new life and may I see the moving of Thy Spirit in mighty power as they did.

AMEN.

Now that you have accepted Messiah Yeshua, secure a copy of the Bible and read from it daily. It will have a complete new meaning for you. (See "Ye Shall Know the Truth" at the beginning of this book; also, "Word of God") Pray daily and ask God to fill you with His Holy Spirit. (See "Holy Spirit")

As never before, you will appreciate and THANK GOD FOR YOUR JEWISH HERITAGE.

"The LORD bless thee and keep thee."

- **John 14:6**- *Jesus saith unto him, I am the way, the truth, and the life: no man cometh unto the Father, but by me.*
- **John 5:39, 40, 46**- *Search the scriptures; for in them ye think ye have eternal life: and they are they which testify of me. [40] And ye will not come to me, that ye might have life. [46] For had ye believed Moses, ye would have believed me; for he wrote of me.*
- **Psa. 118:26**- *Blessed be he that cometh in the name of the LORD: we have blessed you out of the house of the LORD.*

PROPHECY	DESCRIPTION	FULFILLMENT
Micah 5:2	Place of Birth	Matt. 2:1
Isa. 7:14	Virgin Birth	Matt. 1:18

Isa. 11:10	Lineage of David	Luke 2:4
Zech. 9:9	Enter Jerusalem on Donkey	John 12:15
Psa. 41:9	Betrayal by Judas	Mark 14:10
Zech. 13:7	Forsaken by Disciples	Mark 14:50
Zech. 11:12	Price for Betrayal	Matt. 26:15
Zech. 11:13	Disposition of Money	Matt. 27:3-7
Isa. 50:6	Scourging	Matt. 27:26, 30
Psa. 69:19	Shame/ Reproach	Matt. 27:28-29
Psa. 35:11	False Witness	Mark 14:56
Zech. 13:7	Smitten Shepherd	Matt. 26:31
Psa. 22:18	Parting of Garment	John 19:24
Isa. 53:7	Dumb before accusers	Matt. 27:13-14

Isa. 53: 5-6	Crucifixion	Luke 23:33
Psa. 109:24	Fall Beneath Cross	Matt. 27:32
Psa. 69:3	His Thirst	John 19:28
Psa. 69:21	Vinegar to Drink	John 19:29
Psa. 22:17	Stare at Jesus	Matt: 27:36
Psa. 22:16	Pierced hands/ feet	Matt. 27:35
Zech. 12:10	Pierced side	John 19:34
Psa. 22:14	His heart broken	John 19:34
Psa. 38:11	Mother & Friends	Luke 23:49
Psa. 109:25	Mockery of People	Matt. 37:39-40
Psa. 22:7-8, 13	Railing/ Hatred	Matt. 27:39-44
Isa. 53:7	As Lamb of God	John 1:29
Isa. 53:12	As Intercessor	Luke 23:33-34
Psa. 22:1	Intense Cry of	Matt. 27:46

Thus Saith God's Word

	Suffering	
Isa. 50:6	Marred Visage	Mark 14:65
Psa. 22:31	Cry of Victory	John 19:30
Psa. 31:5	Commits Spirit to Father	Luke 23:46
Ex. 12:46	Not a Bone Broken	John 19:33-36
Isa. 53:12	With Transgressors	Luke 23:33
Isa. 53:1-4	Despised/ Smitten of God	Mark 15:29-32
Isa. 53:4-6	Bore infirmities	Matt. 8:17
Dan. 9:26	Messiah Cut off	John 11:50-52
Gen. 3:15	Heel to be bruised	John 13:18
Isa. 53:9	Place of Burial	Matt. 27:57-60
Amos 8:9	Darkness at noon	Matt. 27:45
Psa. 16:10	Raised from Dead	John 20:25-29
Isa. 42:6-8	Light to	Acts 2:47

Thus Saith God's Word

	Gentiles	
Isa. 60:3	Gentiles come to Light	Acts 10:34-35

146

With Middle East tensions nearly at boiling point daily, few people understand the reason for the hatred between these descendants of the first two sons of Abraham, ISHMAEL (father of the Arabs) and ISAAC (father of the Jews). God has promised a son to Abraham and his wife Sarah, both from the line of Noah's son Shem. After years had passed, at Sarah's suggestion, Abraham had a son, Ishmael, by Sarah's Egyptian maid. Thirteen years later, Sarah, miraculously at the age of 90 gave birth to a son, and God said: *"Thou shall call his name Isaac and I WILL ESTABLISH MY COVENANT WITH HIM for an EVERALSTING COVENANT and WITH HIS SEED after him."* (**Gen. 17:19**).

Again at Sarah's insistence, Abraham cast out 16- year old Ishmael and his mother, Hagar, for she said, *"The son of this bondwoman shall not be heir with my son, even with Isaac."* (**Gen. 21:10**).

"and God said to Abraham, 'Hearken unto her voice for in Isaac shall thy seed be called... As for Ishmael, I have blessed him and I will make him fruitful and will multiply him exceedingly and I will make him a GREAT NATION. BUT, my covenant will I establish with ISAAC." (**Gen. 17:20-21**).

God had also promised Abraham: "I will give unto you and your seed after you... the land of Canaan for an everlasting covenant... unto thy see have I given this land, from the river of Egypt unto the great river Euphrates." (Gen. 15:18). When Abraham died, "he gave all that he had unto Isaac."

Now, nearly 4,000 years later and after not having a

country for nearly 2,700 years, God is fulfilling His promise to the Jewish people: "I will take you form among the heather and gather you out of the countries and I will bring you into your own land… of Israel." (Ezek. 35:24, 27:22). Thus, ISRAEL belongs to the JEWS by GOD'S DECREE.

About 610 AD, a young Arab named Mohammed, a descendant of Ishmael, claimed to have had "a vision" in which he was called to be "the last and greatest of the prophets" and he was to spread a new religion (ISLAM) all over the world. It went like wildfire across North Africa, Spain, Southern France , and India as Mohammed and his followers mainly used force. There are now a billion Moslems (Muslims- Mohmmaedans) who pray on their knees three times a day facing Mecca (their holy city in Arabia) and repeat: "There is no god but Allah ad Mohammed is his prophet." Their sacred book is the Koran, containing the words of Allah as taught by Mohammed. (Few know that "Allah" was the name of one of the Quraysh tribal idols in the Kaaba – "House of God" – in Mecca). Islam accepts many of the Old Testament prophets and Jesus was also a prophet.

JESUS COULD NOT HAVE BEEN just a prophet as he would have been a LIAR if He is not the SON of God as He claimed and as He proved to be – having power over the elements, healing the sick, giving sight to the blind, raising the dead, and He, Himself, rising from the dead.

He said: *"I am the way, the truth, and life. No Man comes to the Father but BY ME."* (**John 14:6**) *"I am the door; by me if any man enter in, he shall be saved… The*

*THIEF comes not but for to kill, and to destroy. I AM
COME that they might have LIFE."* (**John 10:10**).

<u>LONELINESS</u>

Everyone feels lonely at times and a certain amount of solitude is essential for the health of the spirit. Actually, though, we are never alone.

- **<u>Psa. 139:7</u>**- *Whither shall I go from thy spirit? or whither shall I flee from thy presence?*
- **<u>John 14:23</u>**- *Jesus answered and said unto him, If a man love me, he will keep my words: and my Father will love him, and we will come unto him, and make our abode with him.*
- **<u>Isa. 41:10</u>**- *Fear thou not; for I am with thee: be not dismayed; for I am thy God: I will strengthen thee; yea, I will help thee; yea, I will uphold thee with the right hand of my righteousness.*
- **<u>Jos. 1:9</u>**- *Have not I commanded thee? Be strong and of a good courage; be not afraid, neither be thou dismayed: for the LORD thy God is with thee whithersoever thou goest.*

God--made you for Himself and only He can fill the void in your life. He longs for you to spend time with Him and return His love.

Invest your loneliness: study His word:

- **2 Tim. 2:15**- *Study to shew thyself approved unto God, a workman that needeth not to be ashamed, rightly dividing the word of truth.*

Spend time in intercessory prayer for relatives, missionaries, friends, people from the newspaper, famous people, those who perhaps have no one else praying for them.

- **Luke 18:1**- *And he spake a parable unto them to this end, that men ought always to pray, and not to faint;*

Use your phone, the mail and personal visits to encourage others. (Read Mat. 25:34-46) *"The harvest is plenteous, but the laborers are few."*

- **2 Cor. 9:6**- *But this I say, He which soweth sparingly shall reap also sparingly; and he which soweth bountifully shall reap also bountifully.*

Let Jesus live with you and through you and you'll never be lonely again.

- **Deut. 31:6**- *Be strong and of a good courage, fear not, nor be afraid of them: for the LORD thy God, he it is that doth go with thee; he will not fail thee, nor forsake thee.*

- **John 14:16**- *And I will pray the Father, and he shall give you another Comforter, that he may abide with you for ever;*

Be sure to take a personal inventory once in a while to see lf you are harboring grudges, jealousy, self-pity, unforgiveness or a complaining spirit as any or all will drive even old friends away and hinder the making of new ones.

Although Jesus is the Divine trash collector, He will not violate one's privacy but waits patiently for it to be brought out (confessed) and relinquished. You can trust Him to take it away no matter what it is as He commands you to be free and clean if you bear His name "Christian", thus representing Him. A radiant countenance and a happy spirit from being right with God draws others to Him.

Most people think they will be completely changed the instant they die and suddenly be made acceptable to God and enjoy eternal bliss in heaven. What a horrendous moment to find it is only a physical change and that their thoughts, desires, likes, dislikes, habits, hates and memories will be theirs FOREVER and that forgiveness and victorious living is ONLY SECURED in this life.

The same is true as to works and rewards for the Christian, to which few give thought. The deadline for doing anything for the Lord, and winning souls comes with the last breath. Nothing can be added and you can be sure God keeps flawless records!

- **Eph. 2:8-10**- *For by grace are ye saved through faith; and that not of yourselves: it is the gift of God: [9] Not of works, lest any man should boast. [10] For we are his workmanship, created in Christ Jesus unto good works, which God hath before ordained that we should walk in them.*

- **2 Cor. 5:10**- *For we must all appear before the judgment seat of Christ; that every one may receive the things done in his body, according to that he hath done, whether it be good or bad.*

- **1 Pet. 1:7**- *That the trial of your faith, being much more precious than of gold that perisheth, though it be tried with fire, might be found unto praise and honour and glory at the appearing of Jesus Christ:*

- **1 Cor. 3:12-13**- *Now if any man build upon this foundation gold, silver, precious stones, wood, hay, stubble; [13] Every man's work shall be made manifest: for the day shall declare it, because it shall be revealed by fire; and the fire shall try every man's work of what sort it is.*

Rewards will consist of crowns, praise and honor from Christ, co-reigning with Him, the size and beauty of mansion, etc. Is it any wonder that Christians are being tested and tried from every side, in every manner and from unbelievable sources? Your love and faithfulness to Him in thought, word, and action have to be proven, not just your giving of money.

Have you truly been loyal enough to Him and His cause to be rewarded and honored by Him? If not, you are still alive and there is still time! Make Him complete Lord of your life and start NOW to lay up treasures in heaven!

<u>MARRIAGE</u>

- **<u>Gen. 1:27</u>**- *So God created man in his own image, in the image of God created he him; male and female created he them.*

- **<u>Gen. 2:18</u>**- *And the LORD God said, It is not good that the man should be alone; I will make him an help meet for him.*

- **<u>Gen. 2:24</u>**- *Therefore shall a man leave his father and his mother, and shall cleave unto his wife: and they shall be one flesh.*

It is man's part to cleave unto (stick to, be united to, remain faithful to) his wife. God planned that they should love, compliment and help Him as well as each other - a triangle, as it were, between heaven and earth. The closer their fellowship to Him, the closer the rela-tionship to each other.

God made Eve from a rib out of Adam's side to walk beside him as a helper and He gave "them dominion over all the works of His hands." It was only a part of the curse, after the eating of the forbidden fruit that Eve was to be subject to Adam.

- **<u>Gal. 3:13, 26-28</u>**- *Christ hath redeemed us from the curse of the law, being made a curse for us: for it is written, Cursed is every one*

> *that hangeth on a tree:* [26] *For ye are all the children of God by faith in Christ Jesus.* [27] *For as many of you as have been baptized into Christ have put on Christ.* [28] *There is neither Jew nor Greek, there is neither bond nor free, there is neither male nor female: for ye are all one in Christ Jesus.*

- **1 Cor. 11:9-12**- *Neither was the man created for the woman; but the woman for the man.* [10] *For this cause ought the woman to have power on her head because of the angels.* [11] *Nevertheless neither is the man without the woman, neither the woman without the man, in the Lord.* [12] *For as the woman is of the man, even so is the man also by the woman; but all things of God.*

Through the ages, God has used both men and women in special ways. He has used women as prophetesses; even as a judge over all Israel. He used a woman to save the Jews from extinc-tion; He brought forth the Savior of the world through a woman and the first person to see the risen Lord was a woman.

As all organizations have to have a head, a presiding officer, so God has appointed the man to be the head of the house.

A wise ruler realizes he is not any authority on every subject and thus delegates responsibilities to knowledgeable people under him who do not run to him for every decision; but use their education, experience, and common sense to accomplish the job for the best of the organization and for his approval.

- **Eph. 5:21, 23-33**- [21] *Submitting yourselves one to another in the fear of God.* [23] *For the husband is the head of the wife, even as Christ is the head of the church: and he is the saviour of the body.* [24] *Therefore as the church is subject unto Christ, so let the wives be to their own husbands in every thing.* [25] *Husbands, love your wives, even as Christ also loved the church, and gave himself for it;* [26] *That he might sanctify and cleanse it with the washing of water by the word,* [27] *That he might present it to himself a glorious church, not having spot, or wrinkle, or any such thing; but that it should be holy and without blemish.* [28] *So ought men to love their wives as their own bodies. He that loveth his wife loveth himself.* [29] *For no man ever yet hated his own flesh; but nourisheth and cherisheth it, even as the Lord the church:* [30] *For we are members of his body, of his flesh, and of his bones.* [31] *For this cause shall a man leave his father and mother, and shall be joined unto his wife, and they two shall be one flesh.* [32] *This is a great mystery: but I speak concerning Christ and the church.* [33] *Nevertheless let every one of you in particular so love his wife even as himself; and the wife see that she reverence her husband.*

- <u>**1 Pet. 3:7**</u>- *Likewise, ye husbands, dwell with them according to knowledge, giving honour unto the wife, as unto the weaker vessel, and as being heirs together of the grace of life; that your prayers be not hindered.*

Who can say which is more important -the positive or

negative in electricity? Nothing electrical works without both in equal amounts. Which is more important, water or air? The man dying in a desert would say water; the drowning person would say air; yet it takes both to sustain life. God has formed both sexes with strong points as well as weak so that each will have a need for and a dependency on the other.

- **1 Cor. 7:3-4**- *Let the husband render unto the wife due benevolence: and likewise also the wife unto the husband. ⁴ The wife hath not power of her own body, but the husband: and likewise also the husband hath not power of his own body, but the wife.*

The man is not superior or always right nor to be a dictator, making all the decisions. (Who is more obnoxious than ANYONE who "runs everything" or is "always right?") Even to Abraham, God said:

- **Gen. 21:12**- *And God said unto Abraham, Let it not be grievous in thy sight because of the lad, and because of thy bondwoman; in all that Sarah hath said unto thee, hearken unto her voice; for in Isaac shall thy seed be called.*

Marriage usually unites two individuals who consider each other intelligent and attractive. Taking vows should not change "lovers" into "competitors" for love is like a crown, when worn by even a poor man, makes him feel like a king on a throne. The fair lady won should be a queen to reign WITH HIM over his household.

- **<u>Matt. 18:19</u>**- *Again I say unto you, That if two of you shall agree on earth as touching any thing that they shall ask, it shall be done for them of my Father which is in heaven.*

Satan fears this strong unity and power of a loving, cooperative, Christian marriage and he fights it from all sides. Both husband and wife should realize they are a TEAM; each encouraging and helping the other; both maintaining team loyalty and standing united against the wiles of the devil who is now breaking up more than one out of every three marriages.

- **<u>Heb. 3:13</u>**- *But exhort one another daily, while it is called To day; lest any of you be hardened through the deceitfulness of sin.*

Most marriage difficulties stem from disobedience to the command:

- **<u>2 Cor. 6:14</u>**- *Be ye not unequally yoked together with unbelievers: for what fellowship hath righteousness with unrighteousness? and what communion hath light with darkness?*

The great number of divorces granted on the grounds of "incompatibility" attest to the folly of selecting a mate without seeking God's choice for the individual. He alone knows everyone's inherited traits, talents, temperament, etc. and the combinations that would work to-gether the most successfully for each individual's happiness and the furtherance of His kingdom on this earth and for eternity.

- **Psa. 127:1**- *Except the LORD build the house, they labour in vain that build it: except the LORD keep the city, the watchman waketh but in vain.*

- **1 Pet. 3:1**- *Likewise, ye wives, be in subjection to your own husbands; that, if any obey not the word, they also may without the word be won by the conversation of the wives;*

Submission does not mean to be a slave to or an employee of, but to submit to the divine order in love; only when that love is returned as Christ loves his church. Thus, a man who loves his wife in this manner would never even think of placing her in a position that would compromise any of God's laws but put her in freedom as set forth in:

- **Proverbs 31:10-31**: *"Who can find a virtuous woman? for her price is far above rubies. [11] The heart of her husband doth safely trust in her, so that he shall have no need of spoil. [12] She will do him good and not evil all the days of her life. [13] She seeketh wool, and flax, and worketh willingly with her hands.[14] She is like the merchants' ships; she bringeth her food from afar. [15] She riseth also while it is yet night, and giveth meat to her household, and a portion to her maidens. [16] She considereth a field, and buyeth it: with the fruit of her hands she planteth a vineyard. [17] She girdeth her loins with strength, and strengtheneth her arms. [18] She* *perceiveth that her merchandise is good: her candle goeth not out by night. [19] She layeth her hands to the spindle, and her hands hold the distaff. [20] She stretcheth out her hand to the poor; yea, she reacheth forth her hands to the needy. [21] She is not afraid of the snow for her household: for all her household are clothed with scarlet. [22] She maketh herself coverings of tapestry; her clothing is silk and purple. [23] Her husband is known in the gates, when he sitteth among the elders of the land. [24] She maketh fine linen, and selleth it; and delivereth girdles unto the merchant. [25] Strength and honour are her clothing; and she shall rejoice in time to come. [26] She openeth her mouth with wisdom; and in her tongue is the law of kindness. [27] She looketh well to the ways of her household, and eateth not the bread of idleness. [28] Her children arise up, and call her blessed; her husband also, and he praiseth her. [29] Many daughters have done virtuously, but thou excellest them all. [30] Favour is deceitful, and beauty is vain: but a woman that feareth the LORD, she shall be praised. [31] Give her of the fruit of her hands; and let her own works praise her in the gates.*

****

Each person has the opportunity to choose a partner; thus each should be happy WITH the choice and MAKE the chosen one happy. Constant encouragement and belief in the man help him battle the business world. Constant tenderness and praise for the wife keeps the never-ending housework from becoming drudgery.

- **Prov. 5:18-23**- *Let thy fountain be blessed: and rejoice with the wife of thy youth. [19] Let her be as the loving hind and pleasant roe; let her breasts satisfy thee at all times; and be thou ravished always with her love. [20] And why wilt thou, my son, be ravished with a strange woman, and embrace the bosom of a stranger? [21] For the ways of man are before the eyes of the LORD, and he pondereth all his goings. [22] His own iniquities shall take the wicked himself, and he shall be holden with the cords of his sins. [23] He shall die without instruction; and in the greatness of his folly he shall go astray.*

****

MARRIAGE is as ESSENTIAL to the preservation of a healthy society as BREAD is the essential "staff of life." NE IT HER is an "INSTANT" production.

Grain must be ground; the ingredients mixed; the dough kneaded and formed into a smooth loaf; followed by a period of "rising;" heat applied; then cooling and at last being cut or broken and served. It takes all of this that one loaf might be made to satisfy man's hunger.

No one lives unto himself or herself .If person-al happiness and fulfillment in life are to be enjoyed, there must be submission to GOD's:

- **grinding and mixing** - blending of two temperaments
- **kneading and smoothing** - dispositions,

selfishness
- **rising**; committed to a warm place before the intense heat is applied - unconditional love and forgiveness
- **in the oven** - trials (finances, job, temptations, in-laws, etc.)
- **cooling** - proving of patience and faith
- **breaking** - giving of one's self without reservation

Although none of these are pleasant, each step is essential in the making of a marriage - that "two might become one" and the children partake of the life-sustaining goodness of a "happy marriage" instead of having lifelong scars from a broken home. (See also "Family").

If a breach has been made, then start mending where you can. You cannot change the heart of another, only God can. Thus stop all blame of others, excusing of self and self-pity; be sure your heart, attitudes and actions are pleasing to God.

- **Prov. 16:7**- *When a man's ways please the LORD, he maketh even his enemies to be at peace with him.*

- **Psa. 37:4-5**- *Delight thyself also in the LORD: and he shall give thee the desires of thine heart. ⁵ Commit thy way unto the LORD; trust also in him; and he shall bring it to pass.*

- **Rom. 12:14, 17-18, 21**- *Bless them which persecute you: bless, and curse not. [17] Recompense to no man evil for evil. Provide things honest in the sight of all men. [18] If it be possible, as much as lieth in you, live peaceably with all men. [21] Be not overcome of evil, but overcome evil with good.*
- **Prov. 10:12**- *Hatred stirreth up strifes: but love covereth all sins.*

(Read 1 Cor. 13:1-7).

DIVORCE, although extremely serious, is not the unpardonable sin. Like all others committed while one was "dead in trespasses and sin;" it leaves deep scars, but it can be forgiven when sincerely repented of and forgiveness sought and accepted. It is not the end of living. GOD HAS NOT DIED nor has HE LOST HIS POWER. He specializes in making a way where there is no way; bringing victory out of defeat. He delights:

- **Isa. 61:3**- *To appoint unto them that mourn in Zion, to give unto them beauty for ashes, the oil of joy for mourning, the garment of praise for the spirit of heaviness; that they might be called trees of righteousness, the planting of the LORD, that he might be glorified.*

God has the answer to every problem. The FIRST requisite is for the individual to be committed to Him. (See "**Salvation**"). The second is to commit the problem to Him, leave it with Him; praising Him and thanking Him for the solution and then waiting patiently for Him. God is never in a hurry (He has to wait on breaking down of human resistance) but when He moves, it is for the good of His child and for His glory. Abraham waited years for the fulfillment of God's promise and God "*counted his believing for righteousness.*"

AFTER a person has laid the foundation of accepting Jesus, (1 Cor. 3:11) "*let every man take heed how he buildeth thereon.*" DIVORCE is NOT ONE of the building blocks and God's word has very definite instructions concerning it.

- **Matt 19:6-10**- *Wherefore they are no more twain, but one flesh. What therefore God hath joined together, let not man put asunder. ⁷ They say unto him, Why did Moses then command to give a writing of divorcement, and to put her away? ⁸ He saith unto them, Moses because of the hardness of your hearts suffered you to put away your wives: but from the beginning it was not so. ⁹ And I say unto you, Whosoever shall put away his wife, except it be for fornication, and shall marry another, committeth adultery: and whoso marrieth her which is put away doth commit adultery. ¹⁰ His disciples say unto him, If the case of the man be so with his wife, it is not good to marry.*

- **Mark 10:11-12-** *And he saith unto them, Whosoever shall put away his wife, and marry another, committeth adultery against her. [12] And if a woman shall put away her husband, and be married to another, she committeth adultery.*

- **1 Cor. 7-10-17, 39-** *And unto the married I command, yet not I, but the Lord, Let not the wife depart from her husband: [11] But and if she depart, let her remain unmarried or be reconciled to her husband: and let not the husband put away his wife. [12] But to the rest speak I, not the Lord: If any brother hath a wife that believeth not, and she be pleased to dwell with him, let him not put her away. [13] And the woman which hath an husband that believeth not, and if he be pleased to dwell with her, let her not leave him. [14] For the unbelieving husband is sanctified by the wife, and the unbelieving wife is sanctified by the husband: else were your children unclean; but now are they holy. [15] But if the unbelieving depart, let him depart. A brother or a sister is not under bondage in such cases: but God hath called us to peace. [16] For what knowest thou, O wife, whether thou shalt save thy husband? or how knowest thou, O man, whether thou shalt save thy wife? [17] But as God hath distributed to every man, as the Lord hath called every one, so let him walk. And so ordain I in all churches. [39] The wife is bound by the law as long as her husband liveth; but if her husband be dead, she is at liberty to be married to whom she will; only in the Lord.*

* * * * * *

THIS LIFE is short at its longest and God's grace is sufficient to endure all things. The companionship and approval of Christ in this life and the next are worth any sacrifice or denying of one's self NOW.

- **Phil. 4:13**- *I can do all things through Christ which strengtheneth me.*
- **Col. 2:9-10**- *For in him dwelleth all the fulness of the Godhead bodily. [10] And ye are complete in him, which is the head of all principality and power:*

LOVE is like a delicate -PLANT that must be cultivated and sheltered to keep it blooming.

LOVE is like a precious GEM that must be guarded that it not be stolen or lost.

LOVE is like FIRE that must be constantly fed that it does not die.

<u>OBEDIENCE</u>

True peace of heart and mind comes only when there is obedience to god's word. Peace and happiness ended in the Garden of Eden because Adam and eve disobeyed god. The world and its inhabitants have not had peace since. God never gives an order or law that is not for the good of man. He did not give the Ten Commandments for his benefit or as a whip but only for man's well-being; to safeguard against all injustice. Peace does not reign where there is adultery, stealing, lying, etc. there would be no wars if all loved god first and their neighbor as themselves.

No matter how much time and money you may give to His work or to charitable organizations, how many meetings you attend, how many prayers you say or how many people pray for you, GOD DEMANDS your obedience. His word gives the rules and, as with anything else, you go by them or you are out.

- **<u>1 Sam. 15:22</u>**- *And Samuel said, Hath*

> the LORD as great delight in burnt offerings
> and sacrifices, as in obeying the voice of
> the LORD? Behold, to obey is better than
> sacrifice, and to hearken than the fat of rams.

- **1 John 2:4**- *He that saith, I know him, and
  keepeth not his commandments, is a liar, and
  the truth is not in him.*

It is impossible to break God's laws of nature without
reaping the effects. Unhappiness, bad health, mental
tension, death and eternal separation from God are the
results of breaking His spiritual laws.
Rom. 2:6-8-

The Christian, as well as the sinner, has to learn to obey
God. Nearly all the difficulties Christians suffer come
from disobedience. If you have disobeyed, ask His
forgiveness and then commence to "bring into captivity
every thought to the obedience of Christ." (2 Cor. 10:5).

And then add your voice with those who declare: "We
will obey the voice of the Lord our God that it might go
well with us and His blessing be upon us," because Jesus
"became the author of eternal salvation unto ALL
THEM THAT OBEY HIM." (Heb. 5:9)

All Christians should obey His "command" to be
baptized in the Holy Ghost. (Acts.1:4) The sinner should
obey His command: "REPENT and BE CONVERTED
that your sins may be blotted out."

<u>PEACE</u>

There never has been a time with more talk a-bout peace than now, and yet less of it. Everyone is searching madly for peace and happiness, for they go hand in hand, and Satan is boldly and cleverly offering his counterfeits - entertainment, liquor, tranquilizers, drugs, free love, false religions, etc., but when his bubbles break, there are only headaches and heartaches left for God says:

- **<u>Isa. 48:22</u>**- *There is no peace, saith the Lord, unto the wicked.*
- **<u>Rom. 5:1</u>**- *Therefore being justified by faith, we have peace with God through our Lord Jesus Christ:*

Satan is ever alert to rob us of this precious commodity.

- **<u>John 16:33</u>**- *These things I have spoken unto you, that in me ye might have peace. In the world ye shall have tribulation: but be of* *good cheer; I have overcome the world.*

- **Isa. 26:3**- *Thou wilt keep him in perfect peace, whose mind is stayed on thee: because he trusteth in thee.*

- **Phil. 4:7-8**- *And the peace of God, which passeth all understanding, shall keep your hearts and minds through Christ Jesus. [8] Finally, brethren, whatsoever things are true, whatsoever things are honest, whatsoever things are just, whatsoever things are pure, whatsoever things are lovely, whatsoever things are of good report; if there be any virtue, and if there be any praise, think on these things.*

- **John 14:27**- *Peace I leave with you, my peace I give unto you: not as the world giveth, give I unto you. Let not your heart be troubled, neither let it be afraid.*

- **Col. 3:15**- *And let the peace of God rule in your hearts, to the which also ye are called in one body; and be ye thankful.*

- **Psa. 34:14**- *Depart from evil, and do good; seek peace, and pursue it.*

- **Rom. 12:18**- *If it be possible, as much as lieth in you, live peaceably with all men.*

- **Prov. 16:7**- *When a man's ways please the LORD, he maketh even his enemies to be at peace with him.*

- **Matt. 5:9**- *Blessed are the peacemakers: for they shall be called the children of God.*

- **Num. 6:24-26**- *The LORD bless thee, and keep thee: ²⁵ The LORD make his face shine upon thee, and be gracious unto thee: ²⁶ The LORD lift up his countenance upon thee, and give thee peace.*
- **2 Pet. 1:2**- *Grace and peace be multiplied unto you through the knowledge of God, and of Jesus our Lord,*

(For World Peace see "Second Coming")

PRAYER

In all parts of the world people have prayed in various manners to all kinds of gods, offering sacrifices, making pilgrimages, repeating prayers, burning candles, even torturing themselves hoping to be hears and to receive an answer for their physical and spiritual needs. Therefore, what GOOD NEWS it is that the KING of KINGS, Creator of all things, has issued a PERSONAL INVITIATION to EVERY PERSON to come at ANY TIME into His presence for a PRIVATE AUDIENCE WITH HIM!

Because of His majesty and power, everyone should bow his or her knees to Him but that is not the only required position. The Bible tells of people who knelt, stood with arms uplifted, prostrated themselves, or prayed while in bed. Jonah prayed in the belly of the great fish and God heard and delivered him!

Jesus instructs us to go directly to God, whom we may address as "Our Father," making our petitions in His name (John 14:13) and "Use not vain repetitions, as the heathen do."

Prayer is a time of:

1. Giving God praise and thanks for His grace, mercy, and love; showing our faith in His Deity and ability.

   - **Heb. 11:6**- *But without faith it is impossible to please him: for he that cometh to God must believe that he is, and that he is a rewarder of them that diligently seek him.*

2. Confessing sins and receiving forgiveness through Jesus as personal Savior.

   - **Isa. 1:18**- *Come now, and let us reason together, saith the LORD: though your sins be as scarlet, they shall be as white as snow; though they be red like crimson, they shall be as wool.*

3. Petitioning for needs and desires for ourselves and others.

   - **James 5:16-18**- *Confess your faults one to another, and pray one for another, that ye may be healed. The effectual fervent prayer of a righteous man availeth much.* ¹⁷ *Elias was a man subject to like passions as we are, and he prayed earnestly that it might not rain: and it rained not on the earth by the space of three years and six months.* ¹⁸ *And he prayed again, and the heaven gave rain, and the earth brought forth her fruit.*

4. Receiving help, peace, joy, and revelation from Him.

5.   Praying *"for them which despitefully use you and persecute you."* (Matt. 5:44).

"I will therefore that men pray everywhere lifting up holy hands without wrath and doubting." "Pray without ceasing... giving thanks."

If your prayers are not answered immediately, "wait patiently for the Lord" for His timing. Also, look to see if anything is wrong in your life that would hinder His answer such as:

1.   Disobedience: (Deut. 1:43-45)
2.   Unconfessed sin (Psa. 66:18).
3.   Indifference (Prov. 1:24-33).
4.   Neglect of Mercy (Prov. 21:13); 1 Pet. 3:7).
5.   Turning from the commandments (Prov. 28:9).
6.   Stubbornness (Zech. 7:11-13).
7.   Instability (James 1:6-7)
8.   Self- Indulgence (lusts) (James 4:3)

We should never forget what a GREAT PRIVILEGE we have to take EVERYTHING to GOD in PRAYER!

PROTECTION

- **Psa. 34:7**- *The angel of the LORD encampeth round about them that fear him, and delivereth them.*

- **Jos. 1:9**- *Have not I commanded thee? Be strong and of a good courage; be not afraid, neither be thou dismayed: for the LORD thy God is with thee whithersoever thou goest.*

- **Psa. 91**- *He that dwelleth in the secret place of the most High shall abide under the shadow of the Almighty. ² I will say of the LORD, He is my refuge and my fortress: my God; in him will I trust. ³ Surely he shall deliver thee from the snare of the fowler, and from the noisome pestilence. ⁴ He shall cover thee with his feathers, and under his wings shalt thou trust: his truth shall be thy shield and buckler. ⁵ Thou shalt not be* *afraid for the terror by night; nor for the arrow that flieth by day; ⁶ Nor for the pestilence that walketh in darkness; nor for the destruction that wasteth at noonday. ⁷ A thousand shall fall at thy side, and ten thousand at thy right hand; but it shall not come nigh thee. ⁸ Only with thine eyes shalt thou behold and see the reward of the wicked. ⁹ Because thou hast made the LORD, which is my refuge, even the most High, thy habitation; ¹⁰ There shall no evil befall thee, neither shall any plague come nigh thy dwelling. ¹¹ For he shall give his angels charge over thee, to keep thee in all thy ways. ¹² They shall bear thee up in their hands, lest thou dash thy foot against a stone. ¹³ Thou shalt tread upon the lion and adder: the young lion and the dragon shalt thou trample under feet. ¹⁴ Because he hath set his love upon me, therefore will I deliver him: I will set him on high, because he hath known my name. ¹⁵ He shall call upon me, and I will answer him: I will be with him in trouble; I will   deliver him, and honour him. ¹⁶ With long life will I satisfy him, and shew him my salvation.*

- **Luke 10:19**- *Behold, I give unto you power to tread on serpents and scorpions, and over all the power of the enemy: and nothing shall by any means hurt you.*

- **Deut. 33:27**- *The eternal God is thy refuge, and underneath are the* *everlasting arms: and he shall thrust out the enemy from before thee; and shall say, Destroy them.*

- **Psa. 121**- *I will lift up mine eyes unto the hills, from whence cometh my help. ² My help cometh from the LORD, which made heaven and earth. ³ He will not suffer thy foot to be moved: he that keepeth thee will not slumber. ⁴ Behold, he that keepeth Israel shall neither slumber nor sleep. ⁵ The LORD is thy keeper: the LORD is thy shade upon thy right hand. ⁶ The sun shall not smite thee by day, nor the moon by night. ⁷ The LORD shall preserve thee from all evil: he shall preserve thy soul. ⁸ The LORD shall preserve thy going out and thy coming in from this time forth, and even for evermore.*

- **Prov. 3:24-26**- *When thou liest down, thou shalt not be afraid: yea, thou shalt lie down, and thy sleep shall be sweet. ²⁵ Be not afraid of sudden fear, neither of the desolation of the wicked, when it cometh. ²⁶ For the LORD shall be thy confidence, and shall keep thy foot from being taken.*

- **Isa. 43:2**- *When thou passest through the waters, I will be with thee; and through the rivers, they shall not overflow thee: when thou walkest through the fire, thou shalt not be* *burned; neither shall the flame kindle upon thee.*

- **Prov. 29:25**- *The fear of man bringeth a snare: but whoso putteth his trust in the LORD shall be safe.*
- **Isa. 59:19**- *So shall they fear the name of the LORD from the west, and his glory from the rising of the sun. When the enemy shall come in like a flood, the Spirit of the LORD shall lift up a standard against him.*
- **Rom. 8:31**- *What shall we then say to these things? If God be for us, who can be against us?*

DEAR FATHER, I claim these promises. I cast fear from me and resist Satan who wants me to doubt Your word; thereby giving testimony against You. Thank You for Your protection thru the blood of Jesus Christ, my Lord. AMEN.

SACRAMENTS

The Lord Jesus gave only two new ordinances and two new commandments to the Church: baptism in water (Mark 16:16), Communion (Luke 22:19), the baptism in the Holy Spirit (Acts 1:4-5; Mark 1:8), and loving one another" (John 13:34). If a person desires to do the will of God, he or she should observe them in obedience and to have a good conscience.

Jesus, Himself, was baptized (Matt. 3:13-17) and us our example. At Calvary He identified with the sinner. In baptism (going under the water), the believer identifies with Jesus in His death and burial, and coming up out of the water with His resurrection. It is an act of obedience and a visible testimony of the invisible transformation that has taken place in the heart.

- **Rom. 6:4**- *Therefore we are buried with him by baptism into death: that like as Christ was raised up from the dead by the glory of the Father, even so we also should walk in newness of life.*
- **Rom. 10:9-** *That if thou shalt confess with thy mouth the Lord Jesus, and shalt believe in thine*

heart that God hath raised him from the dead, thou shalt be saved.

The thief on the cross was saved without baptized. Not realizing it, he complied with the requirements for salvation. He confessed before Jesus ("with his mouth") that he was a sinner; acknowledged Him as "Lord" and, although he saw Him dying, he believed Jesus would live again and have a kingdom. (*"Lord, remember me when Thou comest into Thy kingdom."* (**Luke 23:42**).

Jesus confirmed his salvation: Today, thou shalt be with Me in paradise." This proves that salvation is a gift given when true repentance and faith are demonstrated. IT is not received through baptism nor is it a reward for good works.

The Lord's Supper, Communion) was instigated before the crucifixion, while Jesus was still with His disciples. He told them that the bread and the "fruit of the vine" were symbolic of His death: "This is my body" and "this is my blood"…"This do ye, as oft as ye drink it, in remembrance of Me. For as often as ye eat this bread and drink this cup, ye do show the Lord's death till He comes."

- **1 Cor. 11:27**- *Wherefore whosoever shall eat this bread, and drink this cup of the Lord, unworthily, shall be guilty of the body and blood of the Lord.*
- **1 Cor. 11:29**- *For he that eateth and drinketh unworthily, eateth and drinketh damnation to himself, not discerning the Lord's body.*

- **1 Cor. 11:30-** *For this cause many are weak and sickly among you, and many sleep.*

Who are the "unworthy": (1) everyone who has not had a genuine, life- changing encounter with Jesus; (2) everyone who refuses to put Him first in his life and "overcome the world" (sinful desires, habits, friendships, etc.).

- **Matt. 10:37-38**- *He that loveth father or mother more than me is not worthy of me: and he that loveth son or daughter more than me is not worthy of me. [38] And he that taketh not his cross, and followeth after me, is not worthy of me.*

<u>SALVATION</u>

To lose money, job, health, eyesight, hearing, etc. are great losses but a person's most valued possession is his or her SOUL.

- <u>**Matt. 16:26**</u>- *For what is a man profited, if he shall gain the whole world, and lose his own soul? or what shall a man give in exchange for his soul?*

Therefore, everyone's PRIME INTEREST in life should be the soul's salvation for -

- <u>**Heb. 9:27**</u>- *And as it is appointed unto men once to die, but after this the judgment:*
- <u>**Rom. 14:10, 12**</u>- *But why dost thou judge thy brother? or why dost thou set at nought thy brother? for we shall all stand before the judgment seat of Christ. [12] So then every one of us shall give account of himself to God.*

When the sound -color review of your every thought, word and deed is flashed on the screen, you will be WITHOUT EXCUSE:

"I lived a good life."

- **Rom. 3:12**- *They are all gone out of the way, they are together become unprofitable; there is none that doeth good, no, not one.*
- **Rom. 3:23**- *For all have sinned, and come short of the glory of God;*
- **Isa. 64:6**- *But we are all as an unclean thing, and all our righteousnesses are as filthy rags; and we all do fade as a leaf; and our iniquities, like the wind, have taken us away.*

"I couldn't be saved; I was too bad."

- **Matt. 9:13**- *But go ye and learn what that meaneth, I will have mercy, and not sacrifice: for I am not come to call the righteous, but sinners to repentance.*
- **1 Tim. 1:15**- *This is a faithful saying, and worthy of all acceptation, that Christ Jesus came into the world to save sinners; of whom I am chief.*

"Too many hypocrites in the church."

- **Rom. 14:12**- *So then every one of us shall give account of himself to God.*

"I couldn't have lived it."

- **Phil. 4:13**- *I can do all things through Christ which strengtheneth me.*

"I was working at it; I went to church; paid my debts; I never hurt anyone."

- **Eph. 2:8-9**- *For by grace are ye saved through faith; and that not of yourselves: it is the gift of God: [9] Not of works, lest any man should boast.*

- **Titus 3:5**- *Not by works of righteousness which we have done, but according to his mercy he saved us, by the washing of regeneration, and renewing of the Holy Ghost;*

"I was going to get saved but had things to straighten out first."

- **Prov. 27:1**- *Boast not thyself of to morrow; for thou knowest not what a day may bring forth.*
- **2 Cor. 6:2**- *(For he saith, I have heard thee in a time accepted, and in the day of salvation have I succoured thee: behold, now is the accepted time; behold, now is the day of salvation.)*
- **1 John 1:9**- *If we confess our sins, he is faithful and just to forgive us our sins, and to cleanse us from all unrighteousness.*

"I didn't have time to read the Bible."

You found time for the radio and TV; time to study the manual of laws and regulations to obtain a driver's license. God is just; He gave you 365 24-hour days a year and a manual that you might know His laws:

- **Gal. 5:19-21**- *Now the works of the flesh are manifest, which are these; Adultery, fornication, uncleanness, lasciviousness, [20] Idolatry, witchcraft, hatred, variance, emulations, wrath, strife, seditions, heresies, [21] Envyings, murders, drunkenness, revellings, and such like: of the which I tell you before, as I have also told you in time past, that they which do such things shall not inherit the kingdom of God.*
- **Rev. 21:8**- *But the fearful, and unbelieving, and the abominable, and murderers, and whoremongers, and sorcerers, and idolaters, and all liars, shall have their part in the lake which burneth with fire and brimstone: which is the second death.*

How terrible it would be to hear the Lord say:

"Depart from me, ye cursed, into everlasting fire, prepared for the devil and his angels... there shall be weeping and gnashing of teeth."

Hell was prepared for the devil and his angels for causing the rebellion in heaven and for all the misery on this earth. God made man to be with Him for eternity but He will not force him to do so. Those who reject His

186

offer and follow the devil in this life will also follow him to hell. The choice, therefore, is yours. God has done His part:

- **2 Pet. 3:9**- *The Lord is not slack concerning his promise, as some men count slackness; but is longsuffering to us-ward, not willing that any should perish, but that all should come to repentance.*

- **John 3:16-17**- *For God so loved the world, that he gave his only begotten Son, that whosoever believeth in him should not perish, but have everlasting life. [17] For God sent not his Son into the world to condemn the world; but that the world through him might be saved.*

- **Isa. 53:6**- *All we like sheep have gone astray; we have turned every one to his own way; and the LORD hath laid on him the iniquity of us all.*

- **Rom. 6:23**- *For the wages of sin is death; but the gift of God is eternal life through Jesus Christ our Lord.*

God did not give us a choice as to our parents; their social level; nor country of our birth as earthly ties are soon over but heavenly ones are forever. Thus He gives us the opportunity to choose a new father, a new social level and a new nationality for eternity.

- **John 1:12**- *But as many as received him, to them gave he power to become the sons of*

God, even to them that believe on his name:

- **Gal. 4:4-7**- *But when the fulness of the time was come, God sent forth his Son, made of a woman, made under the law, ⁵ To redeem them that were under the law, that we might receive the adoption of sons. ⁶ And because ye are sons, God hath sent forth the Spirit of his Son into your hearts, crying, Abba, Father. ⁷ Wherefore thou art no more a servant, but a son; and if a son, then an heir of God through Christ.*

- **Rev. 21:7**- *He that overcometh shall inherit all things; and I will be his God, and he shall be my son.*

- **John 3:5-8**- *Jesus answered, Verily, verily, I say unto thee, Except a man be born of water and of the Spirit, he cannot enter into the kingdom of God. ⁶ That which is born of the flesh is flesh; and that which is born of the Spirit is spirit. ⁷ Marvel not that I said unto thee, Ye must be born again. ⁸ The wind bloweth where it listeth, and thou hearest the sound thereof, but canst not tell whence it cometh, and whither it goeth: so is every one that is born of the Spirit.*

Being "born of water" is the physical birth a definite time of coming from darkness into light and newness of life. The "spiritual birth" is just as definite; coming from the "darkness of sin" into the "light of the glorious gospel."

- **2 Cor. 5:17**- *Therefore if any man be in Christ, he is a new creature: old things are passed away; behold, all things are become new.*

Jesus likened the new birth experience" to the wind, which can be heard and felt but not actually seen. We do not see God, nor our sins being erased but when we sincerely repent and confess out sins to Jesus and by faith believe that He has done His part, what a feeling of relief and peace!

- **Rom. 8:16-17**- *The Spirit itself beareth witness with our spirit, that we are the children of God: [17] And if children, then heirs; heirs of God, and joint-heirs with Christ; if so be that we suffer with him, that we may be also glorified together.*

- **Eph. 2:19**- *Now therefore ye are no more strangers and foreigners, but fellow citizens with the saints, and of the household of God;*

What GOOD NEWS! The choice is yours. Jesus extends His nail-pierced hands and tenderly invites you to come to Him.

Wouldn't you like to have all your sins erased; completely forgiven and forgotten by God, and the opportunity to start all over as if you had never sinned? Wouldn't you like to be in a royal family - child of the King? Wouldn't you like to be a citizen of a country where no one will ever be sick, not even have a pain, nor shed a tear, nor grow old; where there will be no more war, nor death but only peace and joy forever with the Creator of the Universe pro-viding everything? You would ... wouldn't you? Tell Him so now.

DEAR GOD. Thank You for letting me live until this moment. If I had died, I would have gone to hell. I repent of my sins; I'm sorry for them and I don't want to sin any more. I want nothing to do with the devil. I choose to be Your child; a citizen of Your kingdom.

JESUS, I accept You as my Savior. I truly thank You for shedding Your blood for my sins a n d for rising from the dead that I, too, may have victory over the grave. I will love and serve You from now on. AMEN.

- **Rom. 10:9**- *That if thou shalt confess with thy mouth the Lord Jesus, and shalt believe in thine heart that God hath raised him from the dead, thou shalt be saved.*

If you sincerely prayed, then believe God did His part and you can confess out loud – "I am saved."

- **Luke 15:10**- *Likewise, I say unto you, there is joy in the presence of the angels of God over one sinner that repenteth.*

As a new-born baby needs food, you must read God's word and pray every day if you are to live and grow spiritually. As a royal child never forget who you are.

- **1 Thess. 5:22**- *"Abstain from all appearance of evil."*
- **2 Cor. 6:17**- *"Wherefore come out from among*

> them and be ye separate, saith the Lord, and
> touch not the unclean thing; and I will receive
> you."

- **James 4:7**- *Submit yourselves therefore to
  God. Resist the devil, and he will flee from you.*
- **Psa. 50:15**- *And call upon me in the day of
  trouble: I will deliver thee, and thou shalt glorify
  me.*

No one wants his or her spouse to be faithful part of the
time, neither does God accept anything less than 100%
faithfulness to Him. "*Ye cannot serve God and
mammon.*" (**Luke 16:13**).

Our Heavenly Father is working on our perfection and
making us "*conformed to the image of His Son... Whom
the Lord loveth, he chasteneth and scourgeth every son
whom he receiveth... If we suffer, we shall also reign
with Him... For we know that all things work together
for good to them that love God, to them who are called
according to His purpose.*"

You are now in the Lord's army and in a real battle with
the forces of evil. (Eph. 6:10-18) You will need to be
"endued with power from on high." (See "Holy Spirit")

Jesus- Our High Priest
Before the coming of Christ, God dealt with His people
(as told in the Old Testament) with examples (pictures)
that would be explained or fulfilled in the New
Testament, such as:

Sin entered into the world through the eating of the fruit
of a tree by a woman.

Jesus, the remedy for sin, came into the world through a woman and died on a tree-(Acts 13: 29)

They took Him down from the tree, and laid Him in a sepulcher.

God said to Moses, "*Thou shalt say unto the children of Israel, I AM hath sent me unto you.*" (**Ex. 3:14**).

In the New Testament, Jesus said: "*I say unto you, Before Abraham was, I AM.*" (**John 8:58**). Then, He finished the sentence: "*I AM the way, the Truth, and the Life.*" (**John 14:6**). "*I AM the Door.*" (**John 10:7**). "*I AM the Good Shepherd.*" (**John 10:14**). "*I AM the Vine.*" (**John 15:5**). "*I AM the Resurrection.*" (**John 11:25**).

God gave the Ten Commandments (the Law) 50 days after the first Passover. (O.T.) The outpouring of the Holy Spirit was 50 days after the resurrection of the Passover Lamb.

In the Old Testament, the priest offered the daily sacrifices, not only for the people, but for himself also because he was not perfect and had infirmities. (Heb.5:2-3).

The Holy of Holies, where resided the Ark of the Covenant, was separated from the rest of The Tabernacle by a veil. Once a year the high priest entered alone to offer the blood for himself and for the sins of the people. (Heb. 9: 9).

Jesus, who was with the Father from the beginning, "*took upon Himself the form of man*" to become the sacrifice and then our High Priest.

- **John 6:38**- *For I came down from heaven, not to do mine own will, but the will of him that sent me.*

- **John 17:4-5, 24**- *I have glorified thee on the earth: I have finished the work which thou gavest me to do. ⁵ And now, O Father, glorify thou me with thine own self with the glory which I had with thee before the world. ²⁴ Father, I will that they also, whom thou hast given me, be with me where I am; that they may behold my glory, which thou hast given me: for thou lovedst me before the foundation of the world.*

- **John 19:17**- *And he bearing his cross went forth into a place called the place of a skull, which is called in the Hebrew Golgotha:*

- **Heb. 9:28**- *So Christ was once offered to bear the sins of many; and unto them that look for him shall he appear the second time without sin unto salvation.*

- **Heb. 10:14**- *For by one offering he hath perfected for ever them that are sanctified.*

- **Matt. 27:50-51**- *Jesus, when he had cried again with a loud voice, yielded up the ghost. ⁵¹ And, behold, the veil of the temple was rent in twain from the top to the bottom; and the earth did quake, and the rocks rent;*

- **Heb. 9:24**- *For Christ is not entered into the holy places made with hands, which are the figures of the true; but into heaven itself, now to appear in the presence of God for us:*

- **Heb.10:12**- *But this man, after he had offered one sacrifice for sins forever, sat down on the right hand of God;*

When God rent the veil of the temple from the TOP to the BOTTOM, he abolished the separation between the two places. It was His invitation to the people (all people) to enter and present their petitions directly to Him without a human intermediary.

- **1 Tim. 2:5-6**- *For there is one God, and one mediator between God and men, the man Christ Jesus; [6] Who gave himself a ransom for all, to be testified in due time.*

- **Heb. 4:15-16**- *For we have not an high priest which cannot be touched with the feeling of our infirmities; but was in all points tempted like as we are, yet without sin. [16] Let us therefore come boldly unto the throne of grace, that we may obtain mercy, and find grace to help in time of need.*

- **Heb. 7:25**- *Wherefore he is able also to save them to the uttermost that come unto God by him, seeing he ever liveth to make intercession for them.*

God made the receiving of His salvation so SIMPLE THAT EVEN A CHILD can UNDERSTAND. It involves only the individual and Himself so that anyone, regardless of location or circumstances, (drowning, lost in the desert, dying on a battle-field, etc,) could call upon Him in the name of His Son and be saved.

- **Acts 2:21**- *And it shall come to pass, that whosoever shall call on the name of the Lord shall be saved.*

Perhaps you think you are not worthy of going directly to Jesus or the Father with you r petition.

- **Ecc. 7:20**- *For there is not a just man upon earth, that doeth good, and sinneth not.*
- **John 14:6**- *Jesus saith unto him, I am the way, the truth, and the life: no man cometh unto the Father, but by me.*
- **John 6:37**- *All that the Father giveth me shall come to me; and him that cometh to me I will in no wise cast out.*
- **John 16:23-24**- *And in that day ye shall ask me nothing. Verily, verily, I say unto you, Whatsoever ye shall ask the Father in my name, he will give it you.²⁴ Hitherto have ye asked nothing in my name: ask, and ye shall receive, that your joy may be full.*
- **Heb. 13:15**- *By him therefore let us offer the sacrifice of praise to God continually, that is, the fruit of our lips giving thanks to his name.*

The Christian's Declaration Of Independence

- I am free from failure for "I can do all things through Christ which strengthen me." Phil. 4:13

- I am free from want for "my God shall supply all my need according to His riches in glory by Christ Jesus." Phil. 4:19

- I am free from fear for "God hath not given us the spirit of fear, but of power, and of love, and of a sound mind." 2 Tim. 1:7

- I am free from doubt for "God hath given to every man the measure of faith." Rom. 12:3

- I am free from weakness, "for the Lord is the strength of my life." Ps. 27:1 and "the people know their God shall be strong and do exploits." Dan. 11:32

- I am free from the power of Satan "for greater is He that is in me than he that is in the world." 1 Jn. 4:4

- I am free from defeat "for God always causeth me to triumph in Christ Jesus." 2 Cor. 2:14

- I am free from ignorance, "for Christ Jesus is made unto me wisdom from God." 1 Cor. 1:30

- I am free from sin "for the blood of Jesus Christ cleanseth me from all sin." 1 Jn. 1:7

- I am free from worry "for I am to cast my cares upon Him." 1 Pet. 5:7

- I am free from bondage "for where the Spirit of the Lord is, there is liberty." 2 Cor. 3:17

- I am free from condemnation, "for there is therefore now no condemnation to them which are in Christ Jesus, who walk not after the flesh, but after the Spirit." Rom. 8:1

Test of a True Believer

1. Believes in Christ as Only Savior:

The true Christian sees nothing but unworthi-ness in himself but has complete confidence that Jesus has forgiven all his sins and has imparted His righteousness to him. He can look forward to death without fear but with anticipation of seeing his Lord. He has complete confidence in God's Word and not in his own fluctuating feelings.

2. Does Not Habitually Sin
   a. A person who is truly regenerated does not commit premeditated sin. Instead, he hates it, flees from it, and fights against it. He cannot prevent occasional wrong thoughts, words, and actions from coming, or shortcomings and omissions. He can say, though, in the sight of God that these things cause him grief and sorrow and he seeks His forgiveness and help.

3. Practices Righteousness
   a. God's child endeavors to do that which pleases Him and to avoid the things God hates: "*A proud look, a lying tongue, and hands that shed innocent blood, [18] An heart that deviseth wicked imaginations, feet that be swift in running to mischief, [19] A false witness that speaketh lies, and he that soweth discord among brethren.*" (**Prov. 6:17-19**).

    b. He continually looks to Christ as his example and can testify: "I am not what I ought to be; not what I want to be; nor what I hope to be; but I am NOT what I USED TO BE and with God's help, I'll become what HE WANTS ME TO BE."

4. Loves Other Christians

• **1 John 3:14**- *We know that we have passed from death unto life, because we love the brethren. He that loveth not his brother abideth in death.*

    a. The born- again believer loves all people, but has a special love for those who are in the same family; are fellow soldiers fighting against the same enemy; are fellow travelers on the same road, headed for the same destination.

5. Overcomes the World.

• **1 John 5:4, 18**- *Whatsoever is born of God overcomes the world... and keeps himself (unspotted from the world."* (**James 1:21**).

    a. The true believer does not mind going against the world's ways, ideas and customs. He fears offending God more than offending man. He resists everything which may lead to sin; using his time, talents, influence end resources profitably; realizing he must give account to God.

(See "Eternal Safety")

(See "Jews" for explanation of Jesus as Savior)

<u>SLEEP</u>

Millions of tranquilizers and sleeping pills are being taken every night to induce sleep but the first requirement for sleep is a clean conscience -confessing and turning from SIN and SINFUL HABITS and releasing of ALL RESENTMENTS.

- **<u>Acts 24:16</u>**- *And herein do I exercise myself, to have always a conscience void to offence toward God, and toward men.*
- **<u>1 John 1:9</u>**- *If we confess our sins, he is faithful and just to forgive us our sins, and to cleanse us from all unrighteousness.*
- **<u>John 1:12</u>**- *But as many as received him, to them gave he power to become the sons of God, even to them that believe on his name:*
- **<u>Psa. 37:7-8</u>**- *Rest in the LORD, and wait patiently for him: fret not thyself because of him who prospereth in his way, because of the man who bringeth wicked devices to pass. ⁸ Cease from anger, and forsake wrath: fret not thyself in any wise to do evil.*

- **Psa. 4:8**- *I will both lay me down in peace, and sleep: for thou, LORD, only makest me dwell in safety.*
- **Psa. 121:3**- *He will not suffer thy foot to be moved: he that keepeth thee will not slumber.*
- **Psa. 127:2**- *It is vain for you to rise up early, to sit up late, to eat the bread of sorrows: for so he giveth his beloved sleep.*
- **Prov. 3:24**- *When thou liest down, thou shalt not be afraid: yea, thou shalt lie down, and thy sleep shall be sweet.*
- **Psa. 3:5**- *I laid me down and slept; I awaked; for the LORD sustained me.*

You cannot serve two masters so "choose you this day whom you will serve." If you are God's child, then trust Him to keep His promise of giving His beloved sleep - natural sleep. Do your part by taking care of your body; getting proper food, (see last page of "Healing") fresh air and exercise.

Some people, on a doctor's advice, take a "little nightcap" to "relax" but God's word consistently condemns the use of alcoholic beverages (see Alcohol) and says: *"Blessed is the man who walketh not in the counsel of the UNGODLY."* (**Psa. 1:1**).

Surely there is no harm in just a little glass to promote drowsiness but a Japanese proverb suns it up well: "A person takes a drink: the drink takes a drink then the drink takes the person." The end results are brain and heart damage, gastritis, pancreatitis, anxiety, malnutrition and depression is more the result of drinking than its cause. It increases the risk of heart disease and cancer.

"My taking a drink is my business. I'm not hurting anyone" are hollow words as family members, friends, business associates and even complete strangers (as in the case of accidents) reap the results.

Within a few minutes after a pregnant woman has drunk liquor, her fetus (unborn child) has had the same drink and it damages the vulnerable developing brain, causing mental retardation, defective vision, stunted growth, disfigurement (a smaller than normal head - a thin upper lip - a short upturned nose - small wide-set eyes - damaged corneas drooping eyelids - twisted bodies), impaired memory, brief attention span and poor judgment.

A great amount of this damage is done in the first 12 weeks, even before the woman is aware she is pregnant and poor innocent children are doomed to LIFE IMPRISONMENT in MISSHAPED BODIES and DAMAGED MINDS. She doesn't have to be an alcohol1c, just one or two drinks a day or 4 or 5 at a time even if done infrequently.

With the widespread, glamorous advertising and the social acceptance of alcoholic beverages, drinking is starting at such a young age, every young woman (even very young girls) should be warned as to these devastating, lifelong effects she can inflict upon her unborn child just through thoughtless acceptance of a few drinks.

France is the heaviest drinking nation in the world and Germans, world champion per capita beer drinkers, down 11 billion liters a year and 20,000 Italians die each year of cirrhotic livers. Drinking has gripped the Russian populace like a snake and Hungarians have doubled their drinking in 30 years but death from liver cirrhosis has risen more than 5 times. Business and the bottle are partners in Japan and now half of Japanese women drink. South Korea consumes more spirits per capita than does any other nation.

Groups promising one-day-at-a-time help for the "recovering addict" and that acknowledge only "a Supreme Power" call it what you want) is NOT THE ANSWER for this enslavement (not disease):ONLY JESUS can completely deliver from liquor's chains and instantly FREE the alcoholic from ever desiring another drink.

"If the SON therefore shall make you free, YE SHALL BE FREE INDEED." (**John 8:36**).

SECOND COMING

The WORLD is SICK! Every newspaper, every radio and TV newscast confirms it. Everything is going wrong everywhere. There is NO PEACE ANYWHERE - between nations, within nations, within cities, within homes, even within the individual. Why? The Prince of Peace, the Creator of all things, has been rejected. His word has been cast aside; His laws broken; His world polluted so that even the fish, the animals, "the whole creation groaneth and travaileth in pain."

Whether man realizes it, or will admit it, he, too, groans for a physical and spiritual escape from it all. There IS a PLAN for ESCAPE for the FEW who will follow instructions. For the rest, everything will go from bad to worse to HORRIBLE!

Jesus is coming to take His true children out; then let the world "go to the devil." Yes, God is going to permit Satan to actually rule in person on this earth.

Although God's prophets foretold many explicit signs of Christ's first coming most people missed Him. Likewise,

God has given many definite signs that point to the second coming of Jesus. Be sure YOU don't MISS HIM!

- **2 Tim. 3:1-4**- *This know also, that in the last days perilous times shall come. ² For men shall be lovers of their own selves, covetous, boasters, proud, blasphemers, disobedient to parents, unthankful, unholy, ³ Without natural affection, trucebreakers, false accusers, incontinent, fierce, despisers of those that are good, ⁴ Traitors, heady, highminded, lovers of pleasures more than lovers of God;*

Jesus said conditions just preceding His return would be "as in the days of Noah." "eating, drinking, marrying," and "the earth filled with VIOLENCE." (Luke 17:26-27) (Gen. 6:12-13).

Their ears were deaf to the warning of God is coming judgment; their only interest was in satisfying the physical; even the violence on every hand did not turn them to God for His help and protection. This is an EXACT picture of today, including VIOLENCE EVERYWHERE.

He said it would also be "as in the days of Lot." (Luke 17:28-30; Gen. 18:20). They were also "living it up" and aside from Lot, no one feared God. It was a city of homosexuals, "All the men of the city, both old and young," who are "abominable" in the Lord's sight, so that He destroyed all but Lot and his two daughters.

The alarming number of homosexuals and their

increased boldness in the last few years is an unmistakable sign of Christ's return.

Daniel, in 534 B.C., wrote that at the time of the end: "many shall run to and fro, and knowledge shall be increased." (Dan.12:4). Crowded airports, highways, etc. attest that people are "on the move!" It took over 5,800 years for man to discover and harness electricity, to invent a car and more for an airplane, but since there has been a "knowledge explosion," not only scientific but never have there been so many schools and students in every country.

- **Matt. 24:7**- *For nation shall rise against nation, and kingdom against kingdom: and there shall be famines, and pestilences, and earthquakes, in divers places.*

ALL these SIGNS are OBVIOUSLY present RIGHT NOW as NEVER BEFORE in history. Even though He said only His Father knew the day and hour of His return, Jesus said a close approximation could be known.

- **Matt. 24:14**- *And this gospel of the kingdom shall be preached in all the world for a witness unto all nations; and then shall the end come.*

(Gospel radio programs are beamed around the world and now gospel television programs are going out to the entire world via satellite.)

- **Matt. 24:32**- *Now learn the parable of the fig*

tree: (**symbolic of the nation of Israel**) *when his branch is yet tender, and putteth forth leaves, ye know that summer is nigh.*

In 1948 God fulfilled His promise to the Jews: "I will take you from among the heathen, and gather you out of all countries, and will bring you into your own land… And I will make them ONE NATION in the land upon the mountains of ISRAEL, and the desolate land shall be tilled, whereas it lay desolate in the sigh of all that passed by." ONLY GOD could KEEP a DEAD, SCATTERED NATION intact for over 2,500 years and bring it to life again. (Ezek. 37) "putting forth leaves." Ezek. 36:24; 37:22; 36:34).

- **Matt. 24:33**- *So likewise ye, when ye shall see all these things, know that it is near, even at the doors.*

Yes, EVERYTHING IS SET for the ESCAPE!

- **Matt. 24:27, 40, 44**- *[27] For as the lightning cometh out of the east, and shineth even unto the west; so shall also the coming of the Son of man be. [40] Then shall two be in the field; the one shall be taken, and the other left. [44] Therefore be ye also ready: for in such an hour as ye think not the Son of man cometh.*

- **1 Thess. 4:16-17**- *For the Lord himself shall descend from heaven with a shout, with the voice of the archangel, and with the trump of God: and the dead in Christ shall rise first: [17] Then we which are alive and remain shall* *be caught up together with them in the clouds, to meet the Lord in the air: and so shall we ever be with the Lord.*

Nothing is ever destroyed, although it may change form; so no matter where or what form a dead body has, God will use it as a seed from which to bring forth the new incorruptible, "glorified" body to unite with the spirit that has already been with Him.

Just before -at the same time -or just after this great event; Russia, E. Germany, Persia, Ethiopia, Libya and Turkey will come down upon Israel (Ezek. 38 &39) and the western confederacy of nations will do nothing but ask questions concerning the move. (Ezek. 38:13) God, however, terminates the war with a tremendous earthquake, huge hailstones and the slaughter of five-sixths of their armies. (Eze.38:18-23; 39:1-19). Their weapons are burned for 7 years- the length of the terrible tribulation which follows.

A world leader (Antichrist) is acclaimed as he "*deceives the whole world… with all power and signs and lying wonders.*" (**2 Thess. 2:9**).

With the Holy Spirit having taken the Church (the Bride) to heaven, God will send His two witnesses: Enoch and Elijah – the only two who have never died ("*It is appointed unto man once to die*" eliminates Moses as one of them).

The Holy Spirit will be "upon" them and ministering in

Thus Saith God's Word

the world in the same manner that He did in the Old Testament period. (Rev.11:3-12).

They shall prophesy 1,260 days (3 ½ years); have power to shut heaven that it rain not…to turn waters to blood, and to smite the earth with all plagues… When they have finished their testimony, the Beast (Antichrist) shall kill them…For 3 ½ days their bodies lie in the streets of Jerusalem. Suddenly they come back to life and ascend into heaven in a cloud.

During this period 144,000 virgin male Jews have been "sealed" and accept Jesus as Messiah, along with a vast number of Gentiles. (Undoubtedly resulting from the testimony of the Two Witnesses) These will all be persecuted (*"Here is the patience and the faith of the saints"*) and martyred. This group of people have to have their faith tested, as have all the rest of children. Many God's Rapture takes place at this time because these are referred to as "saints." The Church-Age "saints" have already been "caught up to be with the Lord." They are not martyred, these are.

The next mention of the 144,000 is when they are singing *"a new song before the throne, having been redeemed from the earth."* (**Rev. 14:3-5**).

At the end of the first 3 ½ years, the devil is forever CAST OUT of heaven and enters into the Antichrist. He is "given power over all kindreds, tongues, and nations" for 3 ½ years.

- **Rev. 12:12**- *Therefore rejoice, ye heavens,*

> *and ye that dwell in them. Woe to the*
> *inhabiters of the earth and of the sea! for the*
> *devil is come down unto you, having great*
> *wrath, because he knoweth that he hath but a*
> *short time.*

- **<u>Rev. 13:16</u>**- *And he causeth all, both small*
  and great, rich and poor, free and bond, to
  receive a mark in their right hand, or in their
  foreheads:

Identification by numbers is widespread. Because of the stealing and losing of credit cards; the danger of carrying cash; possibility of accidently or purposely misapplying funds by computer numbers; the ever-increasing number of checks; a plan is being worked out to replace these with a mark on the individual- preferably on the hand or head!

- **<u>Rev. 14:11</u>**- *And the smoke of their torment*
  ascendeth up for ever and ever: and they
  have no rest day nor night, who worship the
  beast and his image, and whosoever
  receiveth the mark of his name.

He takes over the Jewish temple in Jerusalem and declares himself to be God, "exalting himself above all that is called God, or that is worshipped." He makes was with the remnant of Jews who realize he is not God and that Jesus was their Messiah. They flee to the wilderness where God protects them for 3¾ years. (Rev.12:13-17; Mat.24:15-22; 2 Thes.2:4, 9, 10).

In addition to the "beastly" rule of the Antichrist, God

will pour out His great wrath with unbelievable world-wide catastrophes, including the sun so hot it scorches men; terrible famines and plagues with people "gnawing their tongues for pain," (Rev .16:1-11). The River Euphrates shall dry up so that the vast eastern armies can cross to Israel. (Rev. 9:14-19; 16:12-14).

- **Matt. 24:29**- *Immediately after the tribulation of those days shall the sun be darkened, and the moon shall not give her light, and the stars shall fall from heaven, and the powers of the heavens shall be shaken:*

- **Rev. 16:18-21**- *And there were voices, and thunders, and lightnings; and there was a great earthquake, such as was not since men were upon the earth, so mighty an earthquake, and so great. [19] And the great city was divided into three parts, and the cities of the nations fell: and great Babylon came in remembrance before God, to give unto her the cup of the wine of the fierceness of his wrath. [20] And every island fled away, and the mountains were not found. [21] And there fell upon men a great hail out of heaven, every stone about the weight of a talent: and men blasphemed God because of the plague of the hail; for the plague thereof was exceeding great.*

At the end of this period, the Beast and the armies of all

nations gather together in Israel to make war against Jesus (Rev.19:19; Zech.14:2) who descends from heaven WITH HIS SAINTS (Zech. 14:5; Rev.19:11-19) quickly ends the war (Zech. 14:5-15) casts the Beast and his helper (False Prophet) into the lake of fire; binding Satan and casting him into the bottomless Pit for a thousand years. At last the EARTH has REST as He REIGNS ! over it from Jerusalem for 1,000 years of PEACE! (Zech. 14:20-21; Isa. 11:5-9).

The IMPORTANT thing is TO BE READY for the "ESCAPE" for NO ONE gets to heaven after the rapture without being martyred or dying from hunger, thirst, or exposure to the sun for refusal to take the mark of the beast, as indicated by Rev. 7:14-16.

For any escape, IMPLICIT FOLLOWING of all instructions is imperative. EVERYTHING JESUS SAID was IMPORTANT but many have passed over lightly a very important instruction given in Matt. 25:1-13. All ten virgins (implying purity and separation); all were expecting the bridegroom's arrival; all went out to meet him; all had lamps that were burning: thay all went to sleep; all arose at the announcement of his coming; 5 went in with him to the marriage, but the other 5, in spite of acknowledging him as "Lord" were shut out and head the dreadful statement: "Verily I say unto you, I know you not" (present tense). There was only one difference in the two groups – one had extra oil that their lamps had not gone out. (Oil is symbolic of the Holy Spirit).

What a PATHETIC and TRAGIC SCENE to have been so close, at the very door, expecting the arrival of the one they called "Lord" and having lamps which HAD BEEN BURNING. Surely He would not keep them out for the lack of such a little thing -had they not tried at the last minute to buy more oil?

Between Adam and Noah, many had lived and died believing in and serving God, knowing nothing about an ark. However, when the Flood came, only those who entered the Ark were saved and when the door was shut, no more entered! Through the centuries, people have lived and died believing in and serving Jesus; but to be "alive and caught up" when the Bridegroom comes may require this "extra oil." Therefore, all who consider themselves Christians should search their hearts, their thinking, their believing and sincerely ask the Lord to show them if there is more of the Holy Spirit that they have not received and be willing to humble themselves to receive it, for: "It is better to be safe than sorry." When the Church is raptured, the Bride of Christ is completed and NO MORE WILL BE INCLUDED.

TREMENDOUS POWER, flawless equipment, total dedication put man on the moon. Only the TREMENDOUS POWER of the HOLY SPIRIT, complete CLEANSING of FLESH and SPIRIT, TOTAL DEDICATION will rapture out the believer! "If the Spirit of him that RAISED UP JESUS from the dead DWELL IN YOU, HE... shall also QUICKEN your MORTAL BODIES by HIS SPIRIT that DWELLETH IN you." (Rom. 8:11).

With such evident fulfillment of prophecy up to this point, there is no doubt as to literal fulfillment of the rest. Is there anything or anyone worth holding on to at the expense of missing the Rapture?

- **Mark 8:35-36**- *For whosoever will save his life shall lose it; but whosoever shall lose his life for my sake and the gospel's, the same shall save it. [36] For what shall it profit a man, if he shall gain the whole world, and lose his own soul?*

God doesn't want you to be lost - to be left here.

- **Ezek. 18:23**- *Have I any pleasure at all that the wicked should die? saith the Lord GOD: and not that he should return from his ways, and live?*

Jesus wants you to be with Him. "If I go, I will come again and receive you unto myself; that where I am, there ye may be also." HE WANTS TO BE YOUR SAVIOR, your BAPTIZER in the Holy Spirit and your DELIVERER! If you don't know Him in the first role, you can right now.

DEAR JESUS. In my innermost being I realize this world is on a collision course and I don't want to be in the crash. I want to be in that number when the saints go marching into Your presence. I am not coming to You out of fear or just as an escape but acknowledging my sinful condition and claiming Your blood as my atonement. Forgive me; cleanse me; make me ready for Your coming. Help me to understand about the Holy Spirit for I truly desire all that You have for me. I believe You have saved me. Thank You, Jesus, AMEN.

(See also "Holy Spirit")

- **Luke 21:36**- *Watch ye therefore, and pray always, that ye may be accounted worthy to escape all these things that shall come to pass, and to stand before the Son of man.*
- **1 John 3:3**- *And every man that hath this hope in him purifieth himself, even as he is pure.*

Thus Saith God's Word

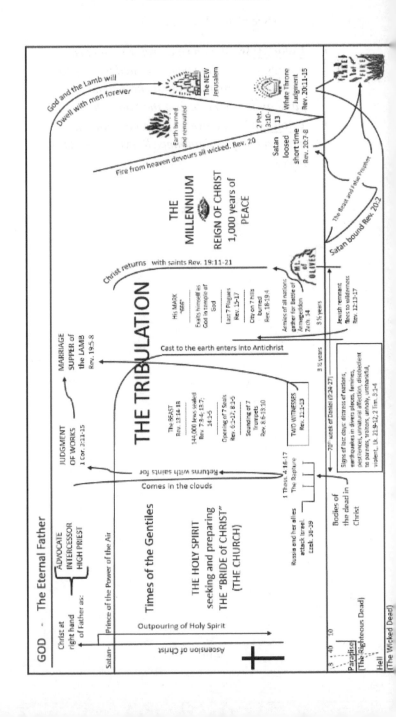

The "tribulation" period is for the purpose of dealing with God's chosen people who have been scattered among the nations while a predominantly Gentile bride for Christ has been chosen (and made ready to rule and reign with Him for 1,000 years) then He "confirms the COVENANT with "thy people" (the Jews) for 1 week." (7 years) Daniel 9:24-27.

The other purpose is to bring to fruition and judgement the evil ECONOMIC systems, the evil corrupt POLITICAL systems, the FALSE APOSTATE RELIGIONS, and all the works of the devil.

The "church" is mentioned 30 times in Rev. 1-3; (not once thereafter – "saints" referring to Jews and others martyred for faith) then begins the "WRATH of the Lamb" "the fierceness and Wrath of Almighty God," etc.

- **1 Thess. 5:9**- *For God hath not appointed us to wrath, but to obtain salvation by our Lord Jesus Christ,*

The Church is to be subject to the governments of the world, therefore cannot be here to be controlled by Satan. (Rev. 13:7). If millions of Christians were still on earth, why would God send "two witnesses" as His special representatives?

Christ returns for Bride as "a thief in the night," "as in the days of Noah… eating and drinking, marrying and giving in marriage. This speaks of normal living conditions which would not be so in the middle of the 7 years and, by no stretch of the imagination, those at the end when men will be scorched by the heat of the sun and calling upon the rocks and mountains to fall upon them.

The Old Testament picture of Christ and His bride is in Genesis. Abraham (God the Father) sent his servant (the Holy Spirit) to seek a wife (the Church) for his son Isaac (Jesus, the Son). Upon Rebekah's acceptance, the servant brought forth jewels of silver and gold (gifts of the Spirit) and then ESCORTED her back to meet Isaac "in the field (clouds) at eventide" and they returned to Abraham's dwelling for the wedding. (Gen. 24).

- **2 Thess. 2:7**- *For the mystery of iniquity doth already work: only he who now letteth will let, until he be taken out of the way.*

This scripture confirms that the Holy Spirit has be "taken out of the way" so "that the wicked one be revealed." "He" cannot possibly refer to a human being for ONLY the HOLY SPIRIT has the POWER to RESTRAIN sin WORLD-WIDE.

In Luke 21:36 Jesus warned: "Watch ye, therefore and pray always, that ye may be ACCOUNTED WORTHY to ESCAPE all these things that shall come to pass, and to stand before the Son of man." "Worthy to escape could not possibly mean "strong enough to flee from" all these things making God's protection dependent upon human strength instead of watching, praying and walking in obedience to God's word so as to "stand before the Son of man" not stand through the tribulation.

It is unbelievable that the multitude of "believers" from the frozen north to the tropics (not ONE PLACE as with Noah and with the Hebrews) could stockpile enough of life's necessities to live WITHOUT the expenditure of ONE CENT for food, fuel, electricity, transportation, etc. (Rev. 13:17), while at the same time God is pouring out the 7 seals, 7 woes, 7 trumpets and 7 vials of His WRATH. The rapture of the church at end of tribulation and immediately eliminates returning to earth for the Battle of Armageddon eliminates the judgement of works, the giving of rewards (1 Cor. 12-15) and the Wedding Supper of the Lamb, (Rev. 19:1-9) the MOST GLORIOUS OCCASION EVER TO TRANSPIRE!

****

There are a few other scriptures that pertain to the Tribulation period that I would like to incorporate for further study.

- Ezekiel 38-39
- Daniel 7
- 2 Thessalonians 2
- Daniel 9:27

SEXUAL SINS

Thru the ages the devil has used the "lust of the flesh" to ensnare even the mighty, including King David and King Solomon. He is working more openly than ever before to trap the young and the old, using pornography (even magazine ads and suggestive clothing), sex films, tele-vision and building up acceptance of pre-marital sex, homosexuality and prostitution. He is out to DESTROY the HOME and the SANCTITY of marriage and the INDIVIDUAL.

- **Gal. 5:19**- *Now the works of the flesh are manifest, which are these; Adultery, fornication, uncleanness, lasciviousness,*

It is impossible to break God's laws without being broken by them. "They that plow iniquity (sin) and sow wickedness, REAP the SAME." (Job 4:8). Venereal disease is raging – 9,000,000 every year are being infected – rich and poor.

- **Num. 32:23**- *But if ye will not do so, behold, ye have sinned against the LORD: and be sure your sin will find you out.*
- **1 Cor. 6:9-10**- *Know ye not that the unrighteous shall not inherit the kingdom of God? Be not deceived: neither fornicators, nor idolaters, nor adulterers, nor effeminate, nor abusers of themselves with mankind, ¹⁰ Nor thieves, nor covetous, nor drunkards, nor revilers, nor extortioners, shall inherit the kingdom of God.*

Adultery (Unfaithfulness in Marriage)

- <u>**Ex. 20:14**</u>- *Thou shalt not commit adultery.*
- <u>**Prov. 6:32-33**</u>- *But whoso committeth adultery with a woman lacketh understanding: he that doeth it destroyeth his own soul. ³³ A wound and dishonour shall he get; and his reproach shall not be wiped away.*
- <u>**Matt. 5:27-28, 32**</u>- *Ye have heard that it was said by them of old time, Thou shalt not commit adultery: ²⁸ But I say unto you, That whosoever looketh on a woman to lust after her hath committed adultery with her already in his heart. But I say unto you, That whosoever shall put away his wife, saving for the cause of fornication, causeth her to commit adultery: and whosoever shall marry her that is divorced committeth adultery.*

- **<u>Mark 10-9, 11-12</u>**- *What therefore God hath joined together, let not man put asunder. And he saith unto them, Whosoever shall put away his wife, and marry another, committeth adultery against her. ¹² And if a woman shall put away her husband, and be married to another, she committeth adultery.*

- **<u>Heb. 13:4</u>**- *Whoremongers and adulterers God will judge.*

Fornication (All sex before Marriage – (See "<u>Covenants</u>").

- **<u>1 Cor. 6:18</u>**- *Flee fornication. Every sin that a man doeth is without the body; but he that committeth fornication sinneth against his own body.*

- **<u>2 Tim. 2:22</u>**- *Flee also youthful lusts: but follow righteousness, faith, charity, peace, with them that call on the Lord out of a pure heart.*

Perversion (Homosexuals and Lesbians)

- **<u>Lev. 18:22</u>**- *Thou shalt not lie with mankind, as with womankind: it is abomination.*

- **<u>Rev. 21:8</u>**- *But the fearful, and unbelieving, and the abominable, and murderers, and whoremongers, and sorcerers, and idolaters, and all liars, shall have their part in the lake which burneth with fire and brimstone: which is the second death.*

- **Rom. 1:24-32**- *Wherefore God also gave them up to uncleanness through the lusts of their own hearts, to dishonour their own bodies between themselves: 25 Who changed the truth of God into a lie, and worshipped and served the creature more than the Creator, who is blessed for ever. Amen. 26 For this cause God gave them up unto vile affections: for even their women did change the natural use into that which is against nature: 27 And likewise also the men, leaving the natural use of the woman, burned in their lust one toward another; men with men working that which is unseemly, and receiving in themselves that recompence of their error which was meet. 28 And even as they did not like to retain God in their knowledge, God gave them over to a reprobate mind, to do those things which are not convenient; 29 Being filled with all unrighteousness, fornication, wickedness, covetousness, maliciousness; full of envy, murder, debate, deceit, malignity; whisperers, 30 Backbiters, haters of God, despiteful, proud, boasters, inventors of evil things, disobedient to parents, 31 Without understanding, covenantbreakers, without natural affection, implacable, unmerciful: 32 Who knowing the judgment of God, that they which commit such things are worthy of death, not only do the same, but have pleasure in them that do them.*

Because sexual sins are being practiced and accepted so openly in these days, it is easy to hide behind the excuse, "Everybody is doing it," "Everybody thinks it is all right," or "It is so sexy!" But GOD SAYS:

- **Isa. 5:20-24**- *Woe unto them that call evil good, and good evil; that put darkness for light, and light for darkness; that put bitter for sweet, and sweet for bitter! 21 Woe unto them that are wise in their own eyes, and prudent in their own sight! 22 Woe unto them that are mighty to drink wine, and men of strength to mingle strong drink: 23 Which justify the wicked for reward, and take away the righteousness of the righteous from him! 24 Therefore as the fire devoureth the stubble, and the flame consumeth the chaff, so their root shall be as rottenness, and their blossom shall go up as dust: because they have cast away the law of the LORD of hosts, and despised the word of the Holy One of Israel.*

Pornography-

- **1 John 2:15-16**- *Love not the world, neither the things that are in the world. If any man love the world, the love of the Father is not in him. 16 For all that is in the world, the lust of the flesh, and the lust of the eyes, and the pride of life, is not of the Father, but is of the world.*

- **Psa. 101:3**- *I will set no wicked thing before mine eyes: I hate the work of them that turn aside; it shall not cleave to me.*

Each person is accountable as to what he or she WILL or WILL NOT look at, listen to, or participate in. Most people are fairly careful and selective of the food they put in their stomachs but put no restraint on the GARBAGE THAT ENTERS their MIND thru the eye and ear gates - corrupting their thoughts. God will not pass this by. He says: "Hear, O Earth; behold I will BRING EVIL upon this people, even the FRUIT of THEIR THOUGHTS."

- **Phil. 4:8**- *Finally, brethren, whatsoever things are true, whatsoever things are honest, whatsoever things are just, whatsoever things are pure, whatsoever things are lovely, whatsoever things are of good report; if there be any virtue, and if there be any praise, think on these things.*
- **Prov. 15:26**- *The thoughts of the wicked are an abomination to the LORD: but the words of the pure are pleasant words.*
- **Isa. 55:7**- *Let the wicked forsake his way, and the unrighteous man his thoughts: and let him return unto the LORD, and he will have mercy upon him; and to our God, for he will abundantly pardon.*
- **Prov. 28:13**- *He that covereth his sins shall not prosper: but whoso confesseth and forsaketh them shall have mercy.*

- **2 Cor. 6:2**- *(For he saith, I have heard thee in a time accepted, and in the day of salvation have I succoured thee: behold, now is the accepted time; behold, now is the day of salvation.)*
- **Prov. 27:1**- *Boast not thyself of tomorrow; for thou knowest not what a day may bring forth.*
- **Prov. 29:1**- *He, that being often reproved hardeneth his neck, shall suddenly be destroyed, and that without remedy.*

Call upon Him now for His forgiveness, cleansing and restoration. He will provide for your every physical, psychological and spiritual need if you will entrust yourself to Him.

<u>SMOKING</u>

Millions are concerned about keeping their cars, clocks, refrigerators, etc. in good working order but daily put poison into their most valuable possession- the body- which is more complex and remarkable that any machine man could ever build. God designed, created and gave man this beautiful gift to be the temple in which His Holy Spirit could dwell with the individual's spirt during its sojourn in this world.

- **<u>1 Cor. 6:19</u>**- *What? know ye not that your body is the temple of the Holy Ghost which is in you, which ye have of God, and ye are not your own?*
- **<u>1 Cor. 3:17</u>**- *If any man defile the temple of God, him shall God destroy; for the temple of God is holy, which temple ye are.*

Nicotine is a very powerful drug causing a sharp release of adrenalin, increasing the heartbeat and raising the blood pressure as certain arteries contract. This continual jolt from nicotine drives the heart to as many as 20 EXTRA BEATS per minute in a heavy smoker and can amount to 10 million EXTRA BEATS every EAR; thus a smoker USES up 1 EXTRA YEAR every 3 ½ years, while the heart is straining and pounding away at clogged blood vessels.

Every year 5 times as many Americans die from nicotine

as are killed in auto wrecks. The number of coronary and vascular deaths resulting from cigarette smoking exceed the combined total from all accidents, suicides, and homicides in this country. Only 1 out of 270 non-smokers will die from lung cancer; 1 out of 10 smokers will. Forty percent of cancers in men and thirty percent in women are cigarette related. The nicotine from one package of cigarettes injected at one time would kill faster than a bullet.

Cigarette smoke contains 19 poisons including: furfural (which is 50 times as poisonous as alcohol, carbon monoxide, cyanide, arsenic, formaldehyde, cresol, etc…)

Smoking depleted Vitamin C in the body causing among other things, the skin to dry and wrinkle. Smokers not only endanger their own health but that of others around them.

Children of smokers have twice the respiratory ills as those of non- smokers.

Use of tobacco in ANY FORM is a useless, dirty, and expensive habit and is definitely a "Lust of the Flesh."

- **1 John 2:15**- *Love not the world, neither the things that are in the world. If any man love the world, the love of the Father is not in him.*
- **Prov. 16:27**- *An ungodly man diggeth up evil: and in his lips there is as a burning fire.*
- **2 Cor. 6:17**- *Wherefore come out from among them, and be ye separate, saith the*

Lord, and touch not the unclean thing; and I will receive you.

- **1 John 1:9**- *If we confess our sins, he is faithful and just to forgive us our sins, and to cleanse us from all unrighteousness.*

DEAR LORD JESUS, I confess all my sins to You, especially this one of using tobacco, which I realize was Satan's chain to keep me captive. Thank You for my body; I am sorry I was defiling it. I relinquish the habit and with Your help, I will never use tobacco in any form again. Cleanse me, through Your blood, of all desire and of all effects it has had upon my body. Make me a clean vessel for Your use. Thank You for hearing and answering.

Immediately destroy all tobacco in your possession; buy no more, accept no more.

- **Rom. 13:14**- *But put ye on the Lord Jesus Christ, and make not provision for the flesh, to fulfil the lusts thereof.*
- **1 Thess. 5:22**- *Abstain from all appearance of evil.*
- **Rom. 12:1**- *I beseech you therefore, brethren, by the mercies of God, that ye present your bodies a living sacrifice, holy, acceptable unto God, which is your reasonable service.*
- **1 Cor. 6:19-20**- *What? know ye not that your body is the temple of the Holy Ghost which is in you, which ye have of God, and ye are not*

your own?[20] For ye are bought with a price: therefore glorify God in your body, and in your spirit, which are God's.

- **2 Cor. 7:1**- *Having therefore these promises, dearly beloved, let us cleanse ourselves from all filthiness of the flesh and spirit, perfecting holiness in the fear of God.*

- **Phil. 4:13**- *I can do all things through Christ which strengtheneth me.*

- **Rev. 21:7**- *He that overcometh shall inherit all things; and I will be his God, and he shall be my son.*

- **Titus 2:12**- *Teaching us that, denying ungodliness and worldly lusts, we should live soberly, righteously, and godly, in this present world;*

- **1 Pet. 1:16**- *Because it is written, Be ye holy; for I am holy.*

Remember…

Tobacco is a filthy weed that from the devil doth proceed. Soils your pockets, spoils your clothes, makes a chimney of your nose." (Benjamin Waterhouse).

<u>SUICIDE</u>

"THE DEVIL MADE ME DO IT" is the true cause of every suicide. He is the instigator of every evil thought and deed. He knows God has con-demned him to the lake of fire to be tormented day and night for ever and ever. Therefore, he is trying to cause as many souls as possible to rebel against God so that they will suffer for eternity with him. He caused the first man born in the world to murder the second one ' his own brother. Thus the Bible warns:

- **<u>1 Pet. 5:8</u>**- *Be sober, be vigilant; because your adversary the devil, as a roaring lion, walketh about, seeking whom he may devour:*

Satan knows there is NO CHANCE AFTER DEATH to get right with God.

- **<u>Heb. 9:27-</u>** *And as it is appointed unto men once to die, but after this the judgment:*
- **<u>Luke 16:22</u>**- *And it came to pass, that the*

beggar died, and was carried by the angels into Abraham's bosom: the rich man also died, and was buried;

The devil causes wars and murders that people might be robbed of their right to live and have an opportunity to receive God's salvation.

SUICIDE is the "MURDER" of one's self.

- **Rev.21:8**- *But the fearful, and unbelieving, and the abominable, and murderers, and whoremongers, and sorcerers, and idolaters, and all liars, shall have their part in the lake which burneth with fire and brimstone: which is the second death.*

To commit suicide is to "jump from the frying pan into the fire," a literal fire with flames: "I am tormented in this flame," with not even a drop of water to quench thirst that will last forever, "Send Lazarus, that he may dip the tip of his finger in water, and cool my tongue."

The soul that goes to hell will never again see a ray of sunlight, "Cast him into outer darkness;" nor hear a note of music or a bird sing· "'There shall be weeping; wailing and gnashing of teeth." (Read Luke 16:19-31).

Satan tries to make people think there is no hell by making a joke of it. All of his false religions deny a literal hell or that it is permanent. Jesus talked more about hell than heaven and he cannot lie, HE IS THE TRUTH.

- **1 John 3:8**- He that committeth sin is of the devil; for the devil sinneth from the beginning. For this purpose the Son of God was manifested, that he might destroy the works of the devil.

Life is a GIFT from God and He loves everyone and is *"Not willing that any should perish but that all should come to repentance."* (2 Pet. 3:9).

You may thinking that no one loves you, but God does:

- **John 3:16**- For God so loved the world, that he gave his only begotten Son, that whosoever believeth in him should not perish, but have everlasting life.

It is no hard to find Him.

- **Rom. 10:13**- *For whosoever shall call upon the name of the Lord shall be saved.*
- **John 6:37**- *All that the Father giveth me shall come to me; and him that cometh to me I will in no wise cast out.*
- **Heb. 7:25**- *Wherefore he is able also to save them to the uttermost that come unto God by him, seeing he ever liveth to make intercession for them.*
- **Isa. 26:3**- *Thou wilt keep him in perfect peace, whose mind is stayed on thee: because he*

trusteth in thee.

He promises an eternity where *"there shall be no more death, neither sorrow, nor crying, neither shall there be any more pain."* **(Rev. 21:4).**

Knowing the end of a life controlled by the devil and what Jesus offers for now and eter-nity, and the great price that He paid-

- **Jos. 24:15**- *choose you this day whom ye will serve."*
- **James 4:7-** *Resist the devil, and he will flee from you.*
- **Rom. 10:13**- *call upon the name of the Lord shall be saved.*

YOU ALONE DECIDE YOUR ETERNAL ABODE.

Jesus stands with outstretched arms of love but He will not force Himself on you -you must invite Him in.

(Prayer)

God, I am sorry I ever thought to destroy the precious gift of life You have given me and the opportunity of spending eternity with You. Forgive me. I renounce all connection with Satan -all sinful habits. Jesus, in the power of Your name, I resist him. Free me from his hold on my life. I invite You into my life. Cleanse me with Your blood -all of my past ---words, deeds, thoughts and even any wrong tendencies I might have inherited.

Remake me into a vessel that will bring honor to Your name. I believe You have forgiven me and saved my soul. Thank You, Jesus -O thank You -for Your great love and mercy -for making me Your child! Help me to walk close to You from this moment on."

-Amen.

THOUGHTS

There is a real battle being waged from the cradle up, to control the human mind. Nearly every waking hour, the devil is bombarding the eye and ear gates, trying to enter and corrupt the thoughts--resulting in evil deeds. He has mental wards and prisons filled. We must realize we are in a war and keep our----defense strong, obeying the commands of our Captain:

- **Isa.26:3**- *Thou wilt keep him in perfect peace, whose mind is stayed on thee: because he trusteth in thee.*
- **Psa. 94:11**- *The LORD knoweth the thoughts of man, that they are vanity.*
- **Phil. 4:8**- *Finally, brethren, whatsoever things are true, whatsoever things are honest, whatsoever things are just, whatsoever things are pure, whatsoever things are lovely, whatsoever things are of good report; if there be any virtue, and if*

there be any praise, think on these things.

- **Prov. 23:7**- *For as he thinketh in his heart, so is he: Eat and drink, saith he to thee; but his heart is not with thee.*

- **Psa. 1:1-2**- *Blessed is the man that walketh not in the counsel of the ungodly, nor standeth in the way of sinners, nor sitteth in the seat of the scornful. ² But his delight is in the law of the LORD; and in his law doth he meditate day and night.*

- **Heb. 4:12**- *For the word of God is quick, and powerful, and sharper than any twoedged sword, piercing even to the dividing asunder of soul and spirit, and of the joints and marrow, and is a discerner of the thoughts and intents of the heart.*

- **2 Cor. 10:5**- *Casting down imaginations, and every high thing that exalteth itself against the knowledge of God, and bringing into captivity every thought to the obedience of Christ;*

- **Psa. 139:23**- *Search me, O God, and know my heart: try me, and know my thoughts:*

Actions have their beginning in the mind, which in turn is the influenced by that which is seen and heard.

One of the greatest influences is music. It is the expression of the innermost being, having vital effect upon the MIND, BODY, and SOUL. IT can entertain, stimulate, soothe, cure, inspire but also CAPTIVATE and CONTROL the very thoughts and ACTIONS of one person, a crowd, or even a nation. The responses are automatic and subconscious, over which the listener has no control. They can be GOOD or EVIL.

TRUE MUSIC CAME FROM GOD as only He could have es-tablished the 7-note scale (number of completion) with the finishing eighth note a repetition of the first. (An illustration of Jesus as "the Beginning and the End.") The 3 divisions of MELODY, HARMONY and RHYTHM are another example of the Triune God-Head. All musical keys, each on a 7-chord structure, progress systematically from one to another, interlocking into a circle.

AS WITH ALL OF GOD'S GIFTS, Satan has turned MUSIC into ONE OF HIS MOST POWERFUL WEAPONS to deceitfully capture and destroy. A disorganized mob can be unified with a rhythmic chant and "rock" concerts create mass hysteria, violence, riots, killings.

GOD CREATED ORDER in the Universe; definite cycles in nature and man is essentially a rhythmical beating - heartbeat, respiration, etc. Loud suggestive lyrics and loud, heavy beat, over a period of time leave the listener with little desire or ability to defend himself or herself, resulting in impaired hearing, in drug addiction, loose morals and high nervous tension.

PLANTS GROW BETTER, cows give more milk and chickens lay better eggs when constructive music is played to them. Three hours of rock music a day shriveled young squash plants, stunted beans, crumpled corn, etc. In less than a month, all having leaned as far as possible away from the speaker. Plants exposed to calm, devotional music mea-sured 2 inches higher than those even grown in silence.

IF IT STUNTS and KILLS PLANTS, what does it do to young people? It promotes degenerate, rebellious teenagers. The illegitimate birth rate has risen 250% with the advent of "rock." Teenage mental breakdown and teenage suicides are at an all-time high.

The SAD and FRIGHTENING FACT is that the devil has PENETRATED the Christian church and home THROUGH MUSIC! To put Christian words to rock-type music spiritual fornication and adultery, which God does not take lightly. *"For their rock is NOT as OUR ROCK."* (**Deut. 32: 31**) *"For who is a ROCK save our GOD?"* (**Psa .18: 31**) "Abstain from ALL APPEARANCE of EVIL" The 3 Hebrew youths refused to bow to the devil's music and JESUS rescued them from the fiery furnace.

Music has always played a vital part in worship. God loves adoration of His people and "inhabits their praises." He, Jesus and the SPIRIT are HOLY and the highest RESPECT in WORD and MUSIC is due Them.

"Sing unto the Lord a NEW SONG: for He hath done marvelous thing; let all the inhabitants of the world STAND IN AWE OF HIM... Let them praise Thy great name; for IT IS HOLY... The Lord is clothed in MAJESTY...Let the beauty of the Lord our God be upon us and not unto us, O Lord, unto THY NAME

GIVE GLORY." (Psalms).

THIS should ALWAYS be the TEST: "If Jesus were standing in front of me (and He is actually always present) would I SING or PLAY it this way? Would I be listening to or watching this?"

Be SELECTIVE with the MUSIC you LISTEN TO and EVERYTHING you WATCH, it is being RECORDED on the COMPUTER you of YOUR for MIND!

<u>WORD OF GOD</u>

Every country, city, school, etc. has to have laws; every game must have rules. God, the Creator of all things, set forth His laws in a book -the Bible -so man would not be in doubt as to His rules. More than that, He sent His only begotten Son to this earth to be the Living Word, confirming that which had been written.

The BIBLE is a "literary" and "mathematical" MIRACLE. Its 66 books were written by men from every level of political and social life -from fishermen, and shepherds to priests, physicians and kings. None of them knew their writings were to be part of a combined work yet every part fits perfectly with every other part.

Every Hebrew and Greek letter (the languages the Bible was written in) stands for a number. The numeric value of a word would be the sum of its letters. Every passage in the Bible teems with numeric designs and features, de-monstrating its inspiration with the certainty of a proposition in geometry. No other piece of literature anywhere in the world is known to contain such amazing numerical construction.

In addition to this, the Bible reveals that God associated different numbers with different doctrines and things.

Sin has a number; as does Redemption, Resurrection, Judgment, etc. From the beginning to end, these numbers remain the same. An example is "7" - Completeness: "7 days in a week" –"7 years of plenty" – "7 years of famine" –"7 times around Jericho" –"Wash in Jordan 7 times."

It is absolutely impossible that some 40 men over a period of 1600 years could have planned these two categories of numeric patterns --design upon design-- interlocking the entire book into one continuous harmonious scheme. There need be no other proof that the whole Bible has but ONE AUTHOR -GOD HIMSELF!

- **2 Pet. 1:21**- *For the prophecy came not in old time by the will of man: but holy men of God spake as they were moved by the Holy Ghost.*

This marvelous book has stood the TESTS of time, archaeology, scientific accuracy, and fulfilled prophecy. Cities and empires have faded away but the Bible remains indestructible despite its many enemies and critics. Its pages have pointed the way for millions thru the ages to find forgiveness, peace, joy and the way to heaven. Is it any wonder the devil has tried in every conceivable way to discredit it, misquote it, and misinterpret it and to keep people from reading, believing, and obeying it?

- **Matt. 24:35**- *Heaven and earth shall pass away, but my words shall not pass away.*

- **Luke 4:4**- *And Jesus answered him, saying, It is written, That man shall not live by bread alone, but by every word of God.*

- **2 Tim. 3:16**- *All scripture is given by inspiration of God, and is profitable for doctrine, for reproof, for correction, for instruction in righteousness:*

- **Heb. 4:12**- *For the word of God is quick, and powerful, and sharper than any twoedged sword, piercing even to the dividing asunder of soul and spirit, and of the joints and marrow, and is a discerner of the thoughts and intents of the heart.*

- **Jos. 1:8**- *This book of the law shall not depart out of thy mouth; but thou shalt meditate therein day and night, that thou mayest observe to do according to all that is written therein: for then thou shalt make thy way prosperous, and then thou shalt have good success.*

- **John 15:7**- *If ye abide in me, and my words abide in you, ye shall ask what ye will, and it shall be done unto you.*

- **Psa. 119:105**- *Thy word is a lamp unto my feet, and a light unto my path.*

- **Isa. 55:11**- *So shall my word be that goeth forth out of my mouth: it shall not return unto me void, but it shall accomplish that which I please, and it shall prosper in the thing whereto I sent it.*

- **2 Tim. 2:15**- *Study to shew thyself approved unto God, a workman that needeth not to be ashamed, rightly dividing the word of truth.*

- **Prov. 13:13**- *Whoso despiseth the word shall be destroyed: but he that feareth the commandment shall be rewarded.*

No other book written has caused thieves to become honest; drunkards to be changed into sober non-drinkers; drug addicts to be freed from their slavery and have their minds and bodies restored; prostitutes to forsake their lives of degradation and become chaste wives and mothers; wayward men to return and be faithful husbands and fathers; murderers to ministers.

- **Rev. 22:18-19**- *For I testify unto every man that heareth the words of the prophecy of this book, If any man shall add unto these things, God shall add unto him the plagues that are written in this book: ¹⁹ And if any man shall take away from the words of the book of this prophecy, God shall take away his part out of the book of life, and out of the holy city, and from the things which are written in this book.*
- **John 20:31**- *But these are written, that ye might believe that Jesus is the Christ, the Son of God; and that believing ye might have life through his name.*

Incredible as it may seem, the CHINESE WRITTEN LANGUAGE is another AMAZING PROOF of the authenticity of the Bible! It is a system of word pictures that originated about 4,500 years ago -after the Great Flood and at the time of the building of the Tower of Babel when God dispersed the people throughout the earth by confusing their language. This group of Noah's descendants moved eastward and for the next 2,000 years developed a remarkable culture. Their word pictures had to depict what would be common knowledge so as to be understood by all.

The character for "CREATE" is a combination of a figure for "dust or mud," "a mouth," "movement or life" and "walking." This is exactly what **Gen. 2:7** states: *"God formed (created) man of the dust of the ground, and breathed into his nostrils (mouth) the breath of life; and man became a living (walking) soul."*

The character for "Devil" is a square for "garden" with a cross through the center of it for "well- watered" plus the symbol for "man" and "secret or private." This conveys exactly what is written in Gen. 2:10; 2:3; and Ezek. 28:13. The devil was in the Garden of Eden form which went out four rivers! He spoke as a man privately or secretly to Eve.

The character for "Tempter" is the figure for the "devil" but drawn "under the cover" of "two trees." Gen. 2:9 tells that in the midst of the garden were two trees – the tree of life and the tree of knowledge of good and evil. The eating of the fruit of the latter was forbidden by God but it was the devil who tempted Eve to eat.

The word for EXAMPLE of PATTERN is a combination of "tree," a "lamb," "eternal" and "water." What a fantastic prophetic picture of the "Lamb of God" (Jesus) who would die on the tree (a cross made from a tree) to provide the eternal WATER OF LIFE! (John 4:14).

These are only a few examples of how the formation of the Chinese written language reflected the original belief of the Chinese people in ONE God, CREATOR of heaven and earth, Whom they praised as a loving heavenly Father. Their picture words told of creation, the fall of Adam, the Flood, etc. 1,000 yrs. BEFORE Moses WROTE the FIRST WORD of Genesis -the first book of the Bible!

In spite of Satan's persecution and killing of translators, distributors and readers of the Bible through the centuries, it has consistently been the "best-seller" of all times. Therefore, he has now changed tactics, offering new, "more understandable", "modern" BIBLE VERSIONS with thousands of words omitted (especially the name of Jesus, the blood, hell, etc.), thousands repositioned or added. The startling and frightening truth is that because it is called a "Bible" hundreds of thousands of copies have been sold to easily-deceived "Christians". At last Satan has been able to ensnare a whole new generation that has never heard the true word by which they will be judged. How it must grieve God and Jesus that so many, so easily, so quickly and so willingly accepted a mutilation of His word.

Through the centuries many outstanding people -kings, queens, statesmen, scientists, athletes, etc. have publicly proclaimed their faith in God and His Son Jesus, such as:

DR. GERHARD DIRKS, father of the modern computer which has effected in some manner nearly every individual on the earth, is one of the most brilliant men in the world, having more than 140 patents for his inventions in Germany, England, The United States, Canada, Argentina, Brazil, Belgium, Italy, Switzerland, France , South Africa, India and Australia.

He was an atheist until he realized that the human mind is a computer where God stores all the information on the individual from the cradle to the grave - every thought, every word, every act; all the things that are seen and heard. When Dirks realized that all the details of his life were registered in his own mind and that they were unchangeable, unalterable and irrevocable, he accepting humbled Jesus himself as Savior, before his Creator. After accepting Jesus as Savior, he said: "If God can change me, a hardhearted, stubborn, driving German business executive, He can change anyone!"

JAMES B. IRWIN, astronaut on Apollo 15, says he was a very dedicated pilot and very proud to have been the first and only test pilot on the world's highest and fastest flying airplane, the YF-12A. Although he believed in God when he was selected to go to the moon, he had be-come a skeptic about His guidance and had lost the feeling of His nearness. He was changed when he got to the moon. He felt an overwhel-ming sense of His presence and the great power of God and His Son Jesus Christ.

When he had a problem and there was not time to ask Houston and receive an answer, he prayed and instantaneously knew the solution. It was not some vague sense of direction but a super-natural sensation of His presence.

Mr. Irwin says that to look at our world from up there has to change a person - fill him with great adoration and appreciation of the creative power of God and His great love. It looked like a beautiful, warm, living object, so fragile and delicate that just; a touch of a finger would cause it to crumble. If He controls the world and the vast universe with such infinite precision, how much more He can guide and protect the person that is surrendered to Him.

"The heavens declare the glory of God; and the firmament showeth His handiwork... He is nigh unto all who call upon Him in truth."

WHAT IS THE TRUE PURPOSE FOR LIFE?

EVERYTHING IS MADE FOR A PURPOSE - a book to be read, a violin to he played, a song to be sung. God made man to be a member of His family and to enjoy forever His companionship, His love and His creation. Thus He did not make him as an angel, a servant, or a puppet, without control over his own thoughts and actions but a "living soul" with the free will to love Him and participate in His great plan or accept the offer of Satan, the angel who desired to be worshiped above God and who was cast down to this earth "to try the souls of men."

The first man, formed from the dust but in the image and likeness of God, disobeyed His command. Instead, he believed Satan's lie and sin en-tered into the human race, making a separation between God and man. For this reason God's only Son had to leave heaven; become a man in order to pay the ransom with His own blood. Thus Jesus is the Redeemer and the bridge between God and man over the abyss of sin. He said: I AM the WAY, the TRUTH and the LIFE, no man comes to the Father BUT BY ME." (Jn.14:6)

God made His plan for redemption so simple that even a child could understand it and accept it. Salvation does not depend on going anywhere or doing anything so that anybody, anywhere, any time - on a desert island, floating in the ocean or dying on a battlefield can call on the name of Jesus, be heard and receive forgiveness.

Many think they are not worthy to go directly to Jesus or the Father, but He promises: *"Him that cometh to me I will in no wise case out."* (**John 6:37**).

GOD is a TRIUNE GOD and MAN is a TRIUNE BEING: SPIRIT, the "God-consciousness," the real person, the breath of life that leaves at death; SOUL, the "self-consciousness," the intellect, memory, loves, dislikes, etc.: and BODY, the "world consciousness," the five senses, the earthly house for the spirit and soul that returns to dust.

A person will never find genuine happiness and the true meaning for life in humanism, evolution, atheism or any philosophy dealing with only the body and soul. Consciously or unconsciously the spirit of man longs for the purpose and fulfillment that is only experienced when the union and communion with the Spirit of God is established.

Thus Saith God's Word;
Scripture Aids for Counseling

Dorothy Mason Weymann

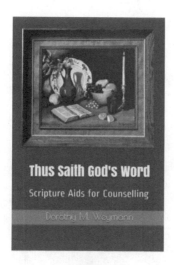

KINGDOM CREATION PUBLISHERS©
Spartanburg, SC

Thus Saith God's Word

**Thus Saith God's Word;
Scripture Aids for Counseling**

Dorothy Mason Weymann

Thus Saith God's Word

Thus Saith God's Word

Made in United States
Troutdale, OR
12/31/2024

27462285R00166